Surviving the Machine Age

Kevin LaGrandeur • James J. Hughes
Editors

Surviving the Machine Age

Intelligent Technology and the Transformation of Human Work

Editors
Kevin LaGrandeur
New York Institute of Technology
New York, New York, USA

James J. Hughes
University of Massachusetts Boston
Boston, Massachusetts, USA

ISBN 978-3-319-51164-1   ISBN 978-3-319-51165-8   (eBook)
DOI 10.1007/978-3-319-51165-8

Library of Congress Control Number: 2017934511

This Palgrave Macmillan imprint is published by Springer Nature
The registered company is Springer International Publishing AG
The registered company address is: Gewerbestrasse 11, 6330 Cham, Switzerland

PREFACE AND ACKNOWLEDGEMENTS

We put this book together because not enough attention is being paid to a technological and economic phenomenon that is hugely important to all of our futures: the increasing displacement of workers by machines. This trend is accelerating, and it threatens not only our livelihoods in the near future, but also, in the long run, the way we identify ourselves, because what we do for work is so often a large part of that identity. Other authors have outlined this problem, but so far few proposals to deal with this situation have been proposed, and they have not been discussed in one place. And the proposals that are available have gained too little attention by policy makers.

This book is an effort to remedy that. The collection of experts on economics, philosophy, law, public policy, and technology in this book picks up where previous authors leave off not only by examining the current state of technologically caused unemployment, but also by providing answers to the question of how we can proceed into a new era beyond this kind of unemployment. Beginning with an overview of the problems, the authors of the chapters in this volume present novel visions of the future and suggestions for adapting to a more symbiotic economic relationship with the artificially intelligent, interconnected machinery that, at the moment, endangers our jobs. The suggestions in this book include unique and new modes of dealing with education, aging workers, government policies, and the machines themselves. Ultimately, many of the authors in this collection lay out a whole new approach to economics, one in which we learn to merge with and adapt to our increasingly intelligent creations.

v

It is our hope that by not only highlighting the problem of technological unemployment here, but by also including a set of answers, we have fashioned a ready reference for those who wish to head off looming social disruption. We also hope that because this volume makes both the problem and the answers accessible, it will inspire our policy makers to take action.

We would like to acknowledge several institutions that have provided support to this project. We would like to express our gratitude to Martine Rothblatt and the Terasem Movement Foundation for a travel grant that helped with the research and development of this volume, and also to the New York Institute of Technology for a small research grant that helped give us time to complete the book.

Our thanks also go to the Oxford University Press, which kindly allowed us to reproduce for Chap. 4 of this volume material that originally appeared in *The Age of Em: Work, Love and Life When Robots Rule the Earth*, by Robin Hanson (Oxford University Press, 2016).

CONTENTS

NOTES ON CONTRIBUTORS

James P. Clark is founder of the World Technology Network (WTN. net), a curated global community of over 1000 of the most innovative people in science and technology peer-elected annually through the World Technology Awards, presented at the close of the annual World Technology Summit. The WTN has also convened the first World Summit on Technological Unemployment. Clark is also the founder of the World Congress for a New Civilization, which will convene delegations from every nation to work together to develop a shared set of principles for a politically/environmentally sustainable twenty-first century.

Educated at Wesleyan University (CT, USA) and Cambridge University (UK), Clark's first venture, a clearinghouse for professional careers in the non-profit sector, was based at Harvard, where Clark was appointed to the faculty at the age 23. In 1992, Clark served in a director-level role for Bill Clinton's successful presidential campaign, after which Clark co-developed the Presidential Transition Roundtable Series. In 1993, he started one of the country's first Internet consulting firms, in partnership with AOL—for which New York Magazine named him a member of "the new media elite." Clark contributes frequently to television on print/ Web-based media, and speaks regularly in venues ranging from the United Nations to Burning Man. He has advised many organizations, including as a founding board member of Teach for America.

John Danaher is Lecturer in the Law School at the National University of Ireland, Galway. He holds a BCL from University College Cork (2006), an LL.M. from Trinity College Dublin (2007), and a Ph.D. from University

College Cork (2011). His research interests lie, broadly, in the areas of philosophy of law, ethics, and emerging technologies. He has published articles on human enhancement, brain-based lie detection, the philosophy of punishment, and artificial intelligence. He maintains a blog called Philosophical Disquisitions, and he also writes for the Institute for Ethics and Emerging Technologies.

David J. Gunkel is an award-winning educator and scholar, specializing in the social aspects of information and communication technology (ICT), with a particular focus on ethics. He is the author of over 40 scholarly articles published in journals of communication, philosophy, interdisciplinary humanities, and computer science. He has published six books—*Hacking Cyberspace* (Westview Press, 2001), *Thinking Otherwise: Philosophy, Communication, Technology* (Purdue University Press, 2007), *Transgression 2.0: Media, Culture and the Politics of a Digital Age* (Continuum, 2011), *The Machine Question: Critical Perspectives on AI, Robots, and Ethics* (MIT Press, 2012), *Heidegger and Media* (Polity, 2014), and *Of Remixology: Ethics and Aesthetics After Remix* (MIT Press, 2016). He has lectured and delivered award-winning papers throughout North and South America and Europe and is the founding co-editor of the Indiana University Press book series Digital Game Studies. Dr. Gunkel currently holds the position of Presidential Teaching Professor in the Department of Communication at Northern Illinois University.

Robin Hanson is Associate Professor of Economics at George Mason University, and Research Associate at the Future of Humanity Institute of Oxford University. He has a doctorate in social science from California Institute of Technology, master's degrees in physics and philosophy from the University of Chicago, and nine years' experience as a research programmer at Lockheed and NASA. He has 2800 citations, 60 publications, 420 media mentions, and he blogs at OvercomingBias. His book *The Age of Em: Work, Love, and Life When Robots Rule the Earth* was published by Oxford in May 2016.

James J. Hughes serves as the Executive Director of the Institute for Ethics and Emerging Technologies (IEET), is a bioethicist and sociologist at University of Massachusetts, Boston where he teaches health policy and serves as Associate Provost, Office of Institutional Research, Assessment and Planning. He holds a doctorate in sociology from the University of Chicago, where he also taught bioethics at the MacLean Center for

Clinical Medical Ethics. Dr. Hughes is the author of *Citizen Cyborg: Why Democratic Societies Must Respond to the Redesigned Human of the Future*, and editor of the 2014 special issue of the *Journal of Evolution and Technology* on technological unemployment.

Kevin LaGrandeur is Professor at the New York Institute of Technology (NYIT), and a Fellow of the Institute for Ethics and Emerging Technologies (IEET). He also has an honors degree in Economics from the University of California. An expert in technology and culture, his recent book *Artificial Slaves* (Routledge, 2013) won a 2014 Science Fiction and Technoculture Studies Prize. He writes extensively about computing and robotics and has been awarded a variety of grants based on his work in this area, as well as for research on computer-assisted instruction and the ethics of robotics.

Gary E. Marchant is Regent's Professor and Lincoln Professor of Emerging Technologies, Law and Ethics at the Sandra Day O'Connor College of Law at Arizona State University. He is also Director of the Program on Governance of Emerging Technologies at the ASU Center for Law, Science and Innovation, Professor of Life Sciences, and Distinguished Sustainability Scientist, all at ASU. Professor Marchant has a Ph.D. in Genetics from the University of British Columbia, a Masters of Public Policy degree from the Kennedy School of Government, and a J.D. from Harvard Law School.

Thomas D. Philbeck is a Global Leadership Fellow at the World Economic Forum in Geneva, Switzerland. He previously served as assistant dean of the College of Arts and Sciences for the New York Institute of Technology, earned a Philosophy Ph.D. from Florida State University, and an MBA from the Hautes Etudes Commerciales (HEC) de Paris. In addition, he is the co-editor of the Handbook of Posthumanism in Film and Television, and has authored several articles/chapters on ontology and posthumansim. He has lived in the USA, UK, Europe, the Middle East, and India, working in various sectors. His area of focus is the intersection between technology, society, business, and philosophy.

Scott Santens has been a moderator of the basic income community on Reddit since 2013. As a writer and blogger, his pieces advocating universal basic income have appeared on such sites as The Huffington Post, the Institute for Ethics and Emerging Technologies (IEET), The Daily Dot, and Quartz. As a basic income speaker, he has presented at the first World Summit on Technological Unemployment and participated as a panelist at the Brookings Institute about the impact of technology on the workforce. As an organizer, he helped plan the first Basic Income Create-A-Thon. He is an advisor to the Universal Income Project, a founding committee member of the nonprofit D.C.-based organization Basic Income Action, a coordinating committee member of the U.S. Basic Income Guarantee Network, and founder of the BIG Patreon Creator Pledge.

Yvonne A. Stevens is a Faculty Fellow of the Arizona State University Center for Law, Science & Innovation (LSI) and sits on its Executive Council board. She also serves as LSI's Community Outreach Coordinator and produces LSI's blog, Bits, Bots & Biomarkers. Her teaching and research focus is on the relationship among, and impact of, law, policy, and ethics within the context of emerging technologies. She received her LL. M. in Biotechnology and Genomics from ASU's Sandra Day O'Connor College of Law in May 2013. She holds an LL. B. (J.D. equivalent) from the Schulich School of Law, Dalhousie University, Halifax, Canada.

Melanie Swan is a Philosopher and Economic Theorist at the New School for Social Research in New York, NY. She is the founder of several startups including the Institute for Blockchain Studies, DIYgenomics, GroupPurchase, and the MS Futures Group. Ms. Swan's educational background includes an MBA in Finance from the Wharton School of the University of Pennsylvania, an MA in Contemporary Continental Philosophy from Kingston University London and Université Paris 8, and a BA in French and Economics from Georgetown University. She is a faculty member at Singularity University and the University of the Commons, and an Affiliate Scholar at the Institute for Ethics and Emerging Technologies. Ms. Swan's career has focused on academic research, finance, and entrepreneurship. She was the Director of Research at Telecoms Consultancy Ovum RHK, and previously held management and finance positions at iPass in Silicon Valley, J.P. Morgan in New York, Fidelity in Boston, and Arthur Andersen in Los Angeles.

LIST OF FIGURES

Introduction: An Overview of Emerging Technology and Employment in the Early Twenty-First Century

Kevin LaGrandeur and James J. Hughes

For two hundred years there have been predictions that technological innovation would lead to widespread unemployment. However, jobs in factories opened as farm work declined, and then jobs in offices and services grew as factory work declined (this process, called "creative destruction," is the topic of James Clark's chapter later in this book). Today we are seeing the rapid transformation of work by robotics, artificial intelligence, the Internet, 3-D (three-dimensional) manufacturing, synthetic biology, and nanotechnology. Automation and other technologies appear to be changing the relative profitability of investments in capital versus labor. In a 2014 survey by Boston Consulting Group (BCG), three quarters of manufacturers expected manufacturing to dramatically improve productivity in the next ten years with the use of robots, materials engineering, digital manufacturing, and 3-D printing (Sirkin et al. 2015).

K. LaGrandeur (✉)
New York Institute of Technology, New York, NY, USA
e-mail: klagrand@nyit.edu

J.J. Hughes
University of Massachusetts Boston, Boston, MA, USA
e-mail: jamesj.hughes@umb.edu

© The Author(s) 2017
K. LaGrandeur, J.J. Hughes (eds.), *Surviving the Machine Age*,
DOI 10.1007/978-3-319-51165-8_1

1

The key question today is whether emerging technologies, especially the exponentially declining cost of information technology, robotics, and automation, will make next couple of decades fundamentally different than the previous two centuries.

Technological Unemployment: The Scope of the Problem

Many economists and policy makers believe that these new technologies will again create as many new jobs as they make obsolete. At most, they believe there will be a need for educational innovation and work re-training to make the transition less painful. They have pointed out (a) that historically innovation has created new employment, (b) that the growth of productivity has actually slowed down in the last 15 years, and (c) that the implementation of IT and robotics has created some forms of employment.

Some recent studies appear to back these claims. A working paper published in May 2016, by the Organization for Economic Cooperation and Development (OECD) claims that if jobs are examined in terms of the collection of tasks within each that are automatable rather than looking at a more general likelihood of automating whole occupations, the likelihood that humans will lose these jobs to robots or computers is not dire: only about 9% in the United States, and the same percentage of jobs across 21 OECD (i.e., developed) countries (Arntz et al. 2016). The authors' rationale here is that we must consider that automation of some tasks in a job does not necessarily lead to the automation of the whole job. Likewise, the VDMA, a German industry trade group for engineering companies, has recently stated that—at least in Germany—there is "no proven correlation between increasing robot density and unemployment, pointing out that the number of employees in the German automotive industry rose by 13 percent between 2010 and 2015, while industrial robot stock in the industry rose 17 percent in the same period" (Prodhan 2016).

Other economists and experts, however, have begun to argue that these innovations may finally create the long predicted decline in work. They point to the dwindling set of skills that humans can still do more cheaply and efficiently than machines, and they are urging policy makers to take seriously the possibility of widespread technological unemployment in the coming decades. These worries are not new, but they are increasing in volume and frequency. One of the first experts to express concern over this issue was economist James Meade, who argued back in 1964, that technological advances would pose a threat to wages (Economist.com 2015).

More recently, preoccupation with the effects of technology on workers has really gained steam because of the increasing danger, and incidence, of labor displacement by intelligent machines. In 2011, for example, two MIT economists, Erik Brynjolfsson and Andrew McAfee, outlined the case for imminent, widespread technological unemployment in their book *Race Against the Machine*, inspiring growing research on the topic. And in a widely cited 2013 study, two Oxford economists, Carl Frey and Michael Osborne, looked at the skill composition of more than 400 jobs in the US economy and weighted the likelihood that each of those jobs would be subject to automation in the next 20 years (*The Future of Employment*). Unlike the authors of the OECD paper noted above, they consider that these jobs all entail enough repetitive or numerical tasks that it is workable to assume their complete automation. Accordingly, they estimated that almost half of all American jobs could be automated in the coming decades. These studies have been replicated with similar results for British (Frey and Osborne 2014) and European occupations (Bowles 2014), as reviewed in Frey and Osborne's 2015 summary of the topic *Technology at Work*. More recently, Martin Ford's book *Rise of the Robots: Technology and the Threat of a Jobless Future* (2015) makes the most contemporary and compelling case. Ford surveys the latest robotics and artificial intelligence innovations in dozens of fields, as they work their way into our factories, roadways, and homes. Without hype, Ford makes clear that a wave of disruption is poised to crash on the global economy.

Statistics from some industry groups support these dire assessments given by authors and experts like Ford. BCG, for instance, in the same report mentioned above that predicts large productivity gains from automation, also projects that within just ten years the rising productivity will lower labor costs and demand for human labor by an average of 16% in the OECD overall, with the largest impacts in South Korea, China, the USA, Japan, and Germany (2015). This forecast is backed by a major technology research firm, Gartner, which recently predicted that software, robots, and smart machines would replace one-third of US jobs by 2025 (Barajas 2014). Given this preponderance of pessimism, there is a need to look more closely at the questions concerning not only whether technological employment will happen, but also at some specific scenarios for it, whether we might avoid it, and some options we may have to do so. Thus, the collection of essays in the present book aims to move the discussion about technological unemployment forward by engaging experts involved in the study of technological unemployment, and by outlining the risks and benefits of the various responses that can be offered if technological unemployment begins to accelerate.

What Types of Workers Are Being Displaced, and How?

Industrial robots began displacing workers in the automobile industry in the 1960s, but now this process is affecting jobs in a much broader way—not just in the working classes, but even in the middle- and upper-middle classes. And this process of technological displacement is accelerating. For example, it may be no surprise, given what has happened in the automobile industry, that the world's first farm that is completely run by robots is about to open in Japan ("World's First 'Robot Run' Farm" 2016b); or that a new Australian robot called "Hadrian" is available for the construction industry, and it can lay bricks 20 times faster than a human. According to an article about it in the online magazine *Techly*, the first model, which is due to be released in 2016, will have "a 28-metre telescopic boom… be mounted on a truck in its final form, [and will use] information from a 3D computer-aided design of the home, with mortar pushed under pressure towards the head of the boom," to lay 1000 bricks per hour (Speight 2015). Of course, the farming robots are likely to displace farm workers, and the bricklaying robots will probably displace masons, which is not unusual. This kind of displacement of manual labor happened in the previous three industrial revolutions as well (the four revolutions are: mechanization/steam, assembly lines/electricity, automation/computers, and cyberphysical systems/interconnected Artificial Intelligence (AI)).

More surprising in today's environment is the breadth of jobs that can be replaced by cyberphysical systems and interconnected AI—the backbone of our current industrial revolution. These interconnected systems that constitute the paradigm shift in today's production replace not only manual laborers but also members of the middle-class, and even highly educated and compensated upper-middle-class workers, and this is a huge difference from past paradigm shifts. In our current revolution, for instance, teleworkers in the service industries are being gradually displaced by automated phone trees; also, more recently, those who interact with customers in digital platforms, such as Twitter and Facebook, are beginning to be replaced by chatbots—AI-based programs that can communicate with customers via text and chat applications. Moreover, increasing numbers of university-educated workers in the financial industries are being replaced by software that can do their jobs faster. Algorithmic trading done by computers in the stock markets is now common, for example, because of which human commodities and equities traders are losing their jobs. Even journalists are being replaced by computer software. In January 2016, "the Associated Press (AP) revealed that [a software program called] Wordsmith has been rolling out content since July 2014 without any human intervention." This Wordsmith software has been generating 1000 stories per month, mostly about financial matters, which is "14 times more than the previous manual output of AP's reporters and editors" (Gleyo 2015). In terms of sheer productivity, humans cannot keep up with ever-faster computers and robots. And even when they can, all things being equal, machines and digital systems are often more convenient and cheaper. A good example of this is the virtual reality real estate tours that are already available at high-end real estate offices in New York City. In those offices, clients can use the newest 3-D virtual reality goggles to view a property in realistic 3-D without even leaving their chairs. For the real estate company, this is cheaper, more convenient, and, at least for now, sexier than employing an old-fashioned human real estate agent to show the property to the client. One real estate office in New York is even showing a property in Brooklyn that has not been completely built yet: the virtual reality program and goggles they use can render a 3-D experience of how the property will look in the future, when it is finished (Miller 2016).

THE CONSEQUENCES TO SOCIETY OF JOB DISPLACEMENT

We need to do something as a society to compensate for our replacement by machines. And we need to start with the workers at the bottom of the labor structure because they will be—in fact, already are being—most immediately affected by technological displacement. As noted above, although workers across the employment spectrum stand to lose their jobs to intelligent machines, the problem is still mainly tied to workers who do manual labor and number-based or repetitive tasks. Jobs that depend on creative solutions to problems or on interacting with and managing people are not as much at risk—though some of the examples mentioned above show that this risk is increasing too. Ultimately, technological unemployment exacerbates the working-class job losses caused by other recent economic changes, such as the offshoring of jobs and the shift from manufacturing to service work. This means that those who do low-wage jobs are the most at risk of being left without any job at all, which will worsen the already increasing gap between the rich and the working poor. This gap is already extreme and getting worse: the most recent State of the Nation's Housing report released on June 22, 2016, by the Harvard University

Joint Center for Housing Studies notes the glum statistic that over the past ten years, 45% of the net growth in the US households has been in those earning only $25,000 or less (Un 2016a). This means almost half of all new households in the United States are below the poverty line.

In past industrial revolutions, this very same situation caused severe social disruptions, from the Luddites rioting in England and smashing steam-powered weaving looms in the early nineteenth century, to America's Haymarket Square riot in 1886, the Colorado Labor Wars in 1903, and the Everett Massacre in 1916. The only thing that eventually quelled violent social disruption was the advent of workers' unions, because this was the only way in which workers could gain power relative to the very wealthy and powerful owners of increasingly automated industries: unionized collective action allowed workers to demand improvement in their conditions. However, in America, at least, unions have waned. Now workers are back to the position of relative powerlessness they suffered about 120 years ago. This combination, namely, increasing downward pressure on wages and job availability caused by automation, the disappearance of avenues for demanding and obtaining improvements in conditions, the concentration of wealth and power in the hands of fewer and fewer people, and the decline in the welfare of all but the top earners in industrialized society, is a repeat of what happened during the so-called Gilded Age. And so we stand in great danger of seeing a repeat of the violence of that era too. We are already seeing some similarities in the teetering of certain social structures: as we write this, Europe is reeling from economic stress, waves of refugees, widespread unemployment, and an increasing income gap—all of which are beginning to mirror the conditions of a century ago. One symptom of this increasing unrest of laborers is the exit of Great Britain from the European Union, which is motivated in great part by the stresses on social structures and the everyday workers just mentioned.

POSSIBLE SOLUTIONS TO TECHNOLOGICAL UNEMPLOYMENT

How do we mitigate the peril of massive unemployment and the poverty, dislocation, and even violence that might follow, as it has in past industrial revolutions? We have four near-term solutions to propose in this chapter as a way to introduce the larger discussion contained in this book and, hopefully, to start a wider discussion of the issues outlined here. These short-term proposals are: cutting back work hours to six hours per day; instituting a Basic Income Guarantee (B.I.G.); instituting micro-fees on certain types of Internet commerce; and using the proceeds of those fees to provide micro-incomes for the rest of society, as well as incentives to open-source developers to provide "bootstrapping" technologies to aid the economically displaced in developed countries and the poor in Third World regions. The following sections elaborate on these ideas.

Reducing Working Hours for Everyone to Provide More Work

The first idea of reducing work hours is already being tried in Sweden. The experiment, based in the city of Gothenburg, and instituted by its City Council, is mainly aimed at reducing worker burnout and illness and at improving working conditions, but businesses have discovered it also has the unexpected benefits of raising productivity and worker efficiency. Reducing all work hours to a maximum of 30 hours per week also makes it necessary to hire more workers, and yet this has been done with surprisingly little increase in cost. This is because workers are more productive and efficient, feeling fresher during their 6-hour days and 30-hour weeks, and so requiring less time to accomplish nearly the same amount of work they did before. Even though the businesses involved do need to hire more workers, the costs of that are offset by productivity gains, so that their bottom line stays healthy. And so do the workers. One example of this successful experiment is Gothenburg's Sahlgrenska University Hospital. According to a recent article in *The New York Times*,

> Last year, the orthopedics unit switched 89 nurses and doctors to a six-hour day. It hired 15 new staff members to make up for the lost time and extend operating room hours. At 1 million kroner (about $123,000) a month, the experiment was expensive, said Anders Hyltander, the executive director. But since then, almost no one calls in sick, and nurses and doctors have been more efficient....The unit is performing 20 percent more operations, generating additional business from treatments like hip replacements that would have gone to other hospitals. Surgery waiting times were cut to weeks from months. (Alderman 2016)

The overall benefits are clear here, but there is a catch. This experiment of reducing work hours has so far been tried mainly in smaller businesses. There have also been some failures, but these failures all have one thing in common: they don't apply the reduced work hours consistently or they don't apply them to the whole workforce. As a result, in the first case, the gains in productivity and efficiency don't happen, and, in the second case, the workers who are not included in the experiment get resentful and workplace friction occurs, reducing productivity. In both of these instances, businesses and workers ended up unhappy. But when applied consistently, the reduction in work hours—and the subsequent hiring of more workers—offers net gains for workers and businesses alike. For our purposes here, the multiplication of job openings for humans by using this strategy would also, importantly, help to offset technological unemployment.

Instituting a Basic Income Guarantee

The second idea, the idea of a Basic Income Guarantee (B.I.G.)—which also goes by other names, such as Universal Basic Income (U.B.I.)—is discussed at length by Scott Santens in a later chapter of this book. His discussion of it focuses on the moral and philosophical reasons it is needed, so here we focus on what it is and how it would work. Let's start with what the idea of B.I.G. offers and where it comes from. The idea of a B.I.G. is not a new one. Thomas Paine first proposed it in his 1797 pamphlet, "Agrarian Justice," as a way to encourage the democratic allotment of common resources and erase the English social hierarchies the new United States had inherited from Great Britain. In his formulation of B.I.G., every person would, when they reach adulthood, receive from the commonwealth the equivalent of £15, about one half the average yearly income of the average laborer. The intent was that they could then use these grants to start them on their way in whatever business they chose. Whereas Paine's intention was to guarantee universal access to opportunity in a society that sought to modify the aristocratic property traditions of its former English overlords, today's version of B.I.G. is slightly different and aimed at ending systemic unemployment.

Here is the way the current notion works: all current social welfare programs—which in the United States would include such programs as unemployment insurance, welfare payments, and food stamps—would be discontinued and replaced by a guaranteed basic income. This would insure that even as human workers were displaced by technology, they would still be able to meet their basic economic needs and they also would not have to worry about the time it would take to re-train themselves for more technological and probably more complex jobs that have a steep learning curve. Finland is, just this year, in 2016, implementing this system. Some smaller regions in other parts of Europe are too, such as the Dutch cities of Utrecht and Tilburg (Boffey 2015). Eighteen more Dutch cities are set to follow their example, and the experiment is also being tried on a very small scale in Germany (only 26 people). In the Dutch experiment, the government will pay the equivalent of $870/month to everyone; anything you earn on top of that you get to keep, whether it is from full time or part time work (Boffey 2015; Sanchez Diez 2015). The obvious worry here, and one that makes the politics of implementing this idea difficult, is that people getting guaranteed income will just sit home watching TV. But there are several things that make this unlikely. First, the amount guaranteed to all is enough to provide necessities, but not so much as to make people feel wealthy; it is similar to social security in the United States, which doesn't kill ambition: many retirees there work, if they are physically able to do so, to fight off boredom, provide extra money, stay socially active, and so forth.

Another consideration is that the present system of forcing people to work short-term menial jobs that they mostly hate discourages them from working, as does the fact that the jobs they find may pay less than their welfare checks, also discouraging them from working. With B.I.G., the intention is that, with no strings attached to the base amount of money one receives, and any extra earned income treated as a bonus, people will be encouraged to find work, and they will also have the time to find—and to train for—work that they like. This would improve things in a number of ways: first, it would reduce the size of the bureaucracy because recipients would no longer be monitored; right now, they are tracked to prove they are doing something in exchange for that money. Second, it would also reduce bureaucracy because just sending people money is far less complex than the current system and can easily be automated (a *good* use of automation). So this system would also be cheaper because of the reduction in the size and complexity of government systems.

Some critics, however, have argued that even these savings would not cover the expenditures necessary for instituting B.I.G. For example, according to the staff of the British business magazine *The Economist,* the recent Swiss referendum to institute a B.I.G. would have been "absurdly expensive: a rough calculation suggests it would cost about SFr197 billion ($210 billion), or 30% of GDP" (Economist.com 2015). Even if their math is correct, there are other ways of boosting the funding for it, or enhancing it, such as generating micro-incomes and/or micro-taxes from previously untapped sources. This brings us to another idea.

Using Micro-Fees and Micro-Incomes to Offset Forced Unemployment

A third idea to combat the declining need for human workers is that of providing a variety of micro-incomes to the general population by levying micro-fees on Internet businesses in exchange for the personal data that they now collect on all of us for free, and also for digital work that such corporations now use for free—such as open-source coding done by unpaid software coders, or other types of work that is resident online. Here is an example: the Google language translation algorithms work by sampling millions of translations created by human translators, but those humans are never paid for that sampling.[1] Similarly, data miners make a lot of money by using data they glean from our Internet use. Why should they get all that from us for free? It would not be difficult to create an algorithm that would credit each of us for use of our property; all those little bits add up. The precedent for this already exists in America where all Alaskans are sent a check at the end of every year for the oil that companies get from their soil.

The fourth and last idea is twofold: to subsidize technology for the economically disadvantaged and to focus on ways to make technology cheaper and more usable for people in poor regions of the earth. This would help those displaced by increasing automation to better keep up with the rapid changes in technology and to make themselves more readily employable in an increasingly digital economy. The second of these two things—making technology more available and cheaper to the Third World—has been in process for a while, as, for instance, in the adaptation of various technologies to energy-poor environments. The examples are windup radios and flashlights; basic laptops like the OLPC XO, a low-cost and low-power laptop computer; and low-cost tech components such as the Raspberry Pi, a small, inexpensive computer processor the size of a credit card that costs only $25–35. The first idea, subsidizing technology like this for the Third World and for the working poor who need technology to re-train themselves for the changing economy, is built into the idea of micro-fees. At least a portion of those fees could be used to subsidize this kind of research into technology for energy-poor, Internet-poor environments; we would suggest that the micro-fees collected from corporations' use of previously free, open-source codes go to this purpose. Right now, all kinds of developers' codes are made available for free by all kinds of hobbyists, and corporations profit handsomely by this.

This amounts not only to corporate freeloading, but worse it is exploitation of the open-source programming community, many of whom live very humble lives. Recently, some of these "citizen developers" have been bucking against this system. Azer Koçulu, for instance, a young man from Oakland, California, with a high school education, deleted the open-source code he had made and posted on the Web for other developers to use as part of a programming template. As detailed in an article in the online magazine *Quartz*, the reason was that a corporation who used his code gave him trouble about the name of his code package: he called the bit of JavaScript he contributed to the template "kik," and an attorney for the messaging application, Kik, emailed him to ask him to change his code package's name, because they needed to protect their trademark (Collins 2016). Because all programmers, including those working for Kik, stood to benefit from his code, because he made and posted it for free, and because he was planning to make an open-source project with the same name, he refused. When Kik became insistent, Koçulu responded by deleting his code, and suddenly lots of programmers around the world—including those being paid good money by digital corporations—could not do their jobs. The issue was ultimately resolved, but this story shows how dependent for-profit entities are on free code contributed to open-source repositories. Why can't corporations pay a small fee, a "donation" to the collective good, every time they use this free material? Why not pay back the altruism of the open-source community by giving back to the wider community?

LONG-TERM SOLUTIONS ARE HARDER TO SEE, BUT THE PAST SHOWS A WAY

We emphasize that solutions like this one and those previously mentioned are only near-term solutions. In the *long run* (and we want to emphasize this, because those who defend automation generally do not distinguish the short-run from the long-run consequences of it) history shows that industrial revolutions spawn a lot of new jobs that evolve from the basis of the revolution itself, from the technology that caused it. We hope that this historical trend continues. One way this is likely to happen is via smart implants in human beings that can leverage the new interconnectivity between and with smart machines. As Thomas Philbeck discusses at more length in his chapter in this volume, humans who agreed to get digital implants to allow enhanced thinking and physical performance could work symbiotically with smart technology in new ways to create whole new employment categories that we have a hard time even imagining now. It is difficult to project very far into the future in any specific way, but the groundwork is already laid for this possibility via a number of emerging innovations.

One such innovation that is already in the prototype phase is a very thin, flexible plastic–metal mesh that is so fine it can be injected into the brain via a large blood vessel, such as the carotid artery. Once in the brain, it unfolds into a sort of microscopic, electronic net that is so thin it becomes assimilated by the neurons of the cortex. Invented by a team of scientists at Harvard, this "syringe-injectable" electronic mesh can be used to record, transmit, or monitor activity in very tiny biological spaces, like those between brain cells. These scientists have already successfully used this very fine, light mesh as a digital device-to-brain interface in mice for transmitting various kinds of information back and forth, and its possibilities for doing the same with humans is clear enough that various groups, including "the U.S. Air Force's Cyborgcell program, which focuses on small-scale electronics for the 'performance enhancement' of cells," have expressed interest (Powell 2015).

What is revolutionary about this innovation is that it can be put into someone's body with an easy, non-invasive injection, as compared to neural electronics used to treat such things as Parkinson's disease—which have to be surgically implanted. Jacob Robinson, a Rice University scientist who develops technology that interfaces with the brain, asserted that this new, neural mesh invention holds huge potential: "This could make some inroads to a brain interface for consumers," he said (Powell 2015). Elon Musk evidently agrees, having said recently that he sees this device—which he calls "neural lace"—as just the kind of thing that will allow humans to interface directly with their digital devices at lightening speed, and so to ramp up their mental power, speed, and capacity in comparison to machines (Furness 2016).

The problem with this kind of long-term solution is one which most of the authors in the present book delve into in their respective chapters: that is, even new solutions to under-employment that the current industrial revolution might provide—such as neural lace—may not be sufficient to resolve the problem of an ever-increasing population in need of work. Even more important, all the authors in our book agree, it would not solve the problem of the increasing chasm between the "haves and have-nots." This is a more fundamental problem that has to do with how we define work, property, ownership, and, especially, the reasons why we work. These issues are the ones that underpin the deeper philosophy of the coming chapters.

OVERVIEW OF UPCOMING CHAPTERS

The second chapter of this book, by Melanie Swan, delves more deeply than this first chapter of ours does into the evidence that technological unemployment is already upon us. She examines how, in our increasingly automated economy, technology has replaced much of the need for non-elective human labor. Thus automation is a double-edged sword. On one hand, technological unemployment worsens income inequality and wealth disparity. On the other hand, there are purported gains in productivity and economic growth. She then posits *Abundance Economics* as a new theory of economics that addresses this problematic disparity in two phases. First, in the automation economy phase, there would be an alleviation of material-goods scarcity for human survival, and second, in the actualization economy phase, there would be a focus on social goods for greater human thriving.

In Chap. 3 James Clark, the Director of the World Technology Network, discusses how "creative destruction"—the notion that new technology destroys older jobs only to create even more new ones—has worked in the past and how it has changed with the present advent of emerging technology in the workplace. He points out in his chapter that in past industrial revolutions, this process of creative destruction worked well; however, this time things look different, mainly because the pace of destruction and change is so much faster and ubiquitous than it was in past revolutions, and that this pace seems to be accelerating. He asserts that there are three big questions we must address now, as a society, in order to prepare for the loss of jobs to smart machines: "1) What are the primary CHALLENGES we likely face regarding these issues in a world heading toward massive technological disruption of human labor? 2) What NEW STRATEGIES regarding these issues would need to be developed/created in order to address these challenges? 3) What ACTIONS should we take now regarding these issues to speed up the move to a stable and equitable society with little required human labor?" He notes that these big questions were tackled for the first time at the recent World Summit on Technological Unemployment held by the World Technology Network and attended by many leaders of industry and economics, and he gives links to their deliberations.

Chapter 4 describes a radically alien future. In it, economist and computer expert Robin Hanson elaborates his theory of what life will be like once we achieve the ability to create human brain emulations—that is, exact, virtual copies of human brains, an event he argues is likely. In the context of the chapter he has written for this book, he discusses how the advent of what he terms "ems" will change the nature of work. He first lays out the reasons he sees ems as a likely near-term phenomenon (i.e., likely to arrive within the next century or so), as opposed to the less likely advent of human-level Artificial Intelligence. Then he describes how whole societies of ems—some in robotic bodies, but most living in idyllic virtual environments—would operate, especially in terms of labor. He goes on to explain how the ems' existence and superior work rates would affect the human employment outlook, leaving humans with two roads to economic happiness: either convert themselves to ems to stretch the wealth that they already have (because living as an em retiree in a virtual existence would be much cheaper than doing so in the physical world), or invest early in ems and in their work.

The fifth chapter examines how technological unemployment will interact with rising old-age dependency and extended longevity. John Danaher opens the fifth chapter of this book by examining how populations in developed societies are rapidly aging: fertility rates are at all-time lows while life expectancy creeps ever higher. This is triggering a social crisis in which shrinking youth populations are required to pay for the care and retirements of an aging majority. Some people argue that by extending the healthy and productive phases of life we can avoid this crisis (thereby securing a "longevity dividend"); however, this chapter argues, this longevity dividend is unlikely to be paid if lifespan extension coincides with rampant technological unemployment. This in turn leads to the argument that our vision of the extended life-postwork utopia may need to be reconceived by prioritizing the role of play and how we conceive of it in the well-lived life.

Chapter 6 asks whether we can build resilience against technological unemployment into future modes of employment. Thomas Philbeck, a philosopher and business specialist who works with the World Economic Forum, presents a number of ways by which experts think we might make future employment more robust. He points to new modes of education, jobs that focus on uniquely human skills, non-standard work (the "gig" economy), new policies and regulations, and even, in the longer term, a merging of humans and machines into a posthuman, hybridized form that might compete with increasingly intelligent machines for jobs. Ultimately, though, he finds something lacking in all of these ideas. Even if humans can digitally enhance themselves, he notes, "If biotechnology becomes the only hope of attaining the high-level skills for high-paying jobs of the future, the division caused by skills-biased technological change will only increase, and then both technology and society will have been thoroughly appropriated by a merely economic orientation." Instead, he concludes that we must "seriously consider that the growth model may not be a desirable end in a technologically mediated society," and that we eventually need to re-define how the economy, society, and individual relate to one another.

U.B.I. is the topic of Chap. 7. In this chapter, Scott Santens makes an impassioned plea for the idea of instituting a U.B.I. (also known by other names, such as Basic Income Guarantee) as a solution to the increasing number of people being put out of jobs because of automation. Key to his argument is his explication of the idea of the "commonwealth" and its obligations: his idea that since all goods and services are produced not in isolation, but by all who make up the economy in general, and that since the wealthy among us therefore benefit greatly from the commons, and that, in addition, because automation stands to provide virtually infinite productivity, everyone deserves a minimal amount of livable income.

Chapter 8 is about policy responses to technological unemployment. Beginning with a survey of various proposed public policies intended to respond to growing technological unemployment, Yvonne Stevens and Gary Marchant, legal specialists on the governance of emerging technology, find them lacking. Instead, they propose that because we likely face an increasingly jobless future in which machines increasingly take over production from human laborers, we need a new system of rewards to replace our standard idea of work. This system would be one comprised of rewards based on a digital "badge" system, where people who may be under-employed would be rewarded, in addition to any income they might earn, with badges that could be traded for supplemental goods and services they might need. These badges could also be used in case automation leads to a situation of abundance, in which money ceases to be meaningful. In either case, badges would be rewarded for activity that society deems meaningful: child-care, volunteer work, or creative production of open-source software, for instance. In this way, people would receive compensation for activities that they like to do and that help society. Marchant and Stevens point to the precedent of China, which is already working on such a system, and where by 2020, "everyone...will be registered in a national 'social credit' database." And they close by giving answers to some possible problems that such a system might raise.

James Hughes assesses the job creation potential of new technologies in Chap. 9. Although most human mental and physical labor will eventually be replaced by automation, complex cognitive skills, such as creativity and social-emotional intelligence, will take longer to replace. As a consequence, there may be, for a time, expanding employment opportunities for occupations that use more of those skills, such as architects, artists and designers, information specialists, and public relations professionals. It is impossible to predict exactly what new creative or social jobs might be invented, but it is likely that the future job market will see more part-time "gig" jobs, public sector jobs, and elder-care jobs, and that many new jobs will be types that will integrate technology, such as the neural lace mentioned above in this introductory chapter, and humans in a symbiotic way.

In the final chapter, philosopher David Gunkel deliberates about how we can re-think education in the face of growing displacement of workers due to technology. The possibility of a future in which automation causes joblessness challenges the existing standard operating presumptions of higher education and the task of preparing and credentialing individuals for employment. This chapter argues for a significant re-calibration of higher education to meet the demands of the twenty-first century by diagnosing the opportunities and challenges that emerging technology presents to existing instructional structures and methodologies, and then by describing concrete steps that can be instituted by both educational institutions and individual students in order to better anticipate and respond to the coming wave of technological unemployment.

NOTE

1. Jaron Lanier discussed this idea at a recent debate: "Don't Trust the Promise of Artificial Intelligence, a debate co-presented with Intelligence Squared U.S." (Wed, Mar 9, 2016, 7 p.m.: Kaufmann Concert Hall, New York, NY). It clearly stems from his earlier ideas regarding automatic, small person-to-person payments for music and other creative content posted on the Internet, which he discusses in his book *You Are Not a Gadget* (2010, 100–101).

REFERENCES

Alderman, Liz. 2016. In Sweden, an Experiment Turns Shorter Workweek into Bigger Gains. *New York Times*, May 20, International Business sec. http://www.nytimes.com/2016/05/21/business/international/in-sweden-an-experiment-turns-shorter-workdays-into-bigger-gains.html?action=click&pgtype=Homepage&version=Moth-Visible&moduleDetail=inside-nyt-region-5&module=inside-nyt-region&region=inside-nyt-region&WT.nav=inside-nyt-region

Arntz, Melanie, Terry Gregory, and Ulrich Zeirahn. 2016. The Risk of Automation for Jobs in OECD Countries: A Comparative Analysis. *OECD Social, Employment and Migration*. Working Papers, No. 189. Paris: OECD Publishing. doi: http://dx.doi.org/10.1787/5jlz9h56dvq7-en

Barajas, Joshua. 2014. Smart Robots Will Take Over a Third of Jobs by 2025, Gartner Says. *PBS Newshour: The Rundown*, October 7. http://www.pbs.org/newshour/rundown/smart-robots-will-take-third-jobs-2025-gartner-says/

Boffey, Daniel. 2015. Dutch City Plans to Pay Citizens a 'Basic Income', and Greens Say It Could Work in the UK. *The Guardian*, December 26. http://www.theguardian.com/world/2015/dec/26/dutch-city-utrecht-basic-income-uk-greens

Boston Consulting Group. 2015. *Takeoff in Robotics Will Power the Next Productivity Surge in Manufacturing*, February 10. http://www.bcg.com/d/press/10feb2015-robotics-power-productivity-surge-manufacturing-838

Bowles, Jeremy. 2014. The Computerisation of European Jobs. *Bruegel Think Tank (Blog)*, July 24, http://www.bruegel.org/nc/blog/detail/article/1394-the-computerisation-of-european-jobs

Brynjolfsson, Erik and Andrew McAfee. 2011. *Race Against the Machine*, Kindle edition. Digital Frontier Press.

Collins, Keith. 2016. How One Programmer Broke the Internet by Deleting a Tiny Piece of Code. *Quartz*, March 27. http://qz.com/646467/how-one-programmer-broke-the-internet-by-deleting-a-tiny-piece-of-code/?utm_source=pocket&utm_medium=email&utm_campaign=pockethits

Economist.com. 2015. Basically Unaffordable. *The Economist*, May 23. http://www.economist.com/news/finance-and-economics/21651897-replacing-welfare-payments-basic-income-all-alluring

Ford, Martin. 2015. *Rise of the Robots: Technology and the Threat of a Jobless Future*. New York: Basic Books.

Frey, Carl Benedikt, and Michael A. Osborne. 2013. *The Future of Employment: How Susceptible Are Jobs to Computerisation?* Oxford: Oxford Martin School Working Paper.

———. 2014. Agiletown: The Relentless March of Technology and London's Response. *London Futures*. Deloitte, November. http://www2.deloitte.com/uk/en/pages/growth/articles/agiletown-the-relentless-march-of-technology-and-londons-response.html#

———. 2015. *Technology at Work: The Future of Innovation and Employment*. Oxford: Oxford Martin School.

Furness, Dyllan. 2016. Elon Musk Thinks We Should Insert 'Neural Laces' into Our Brains So We Can Become Cyborgs. *Digital Trends*, June 3. http://www.digitaltrends.com/cool-tech/elon-musk-cyborg/

Gleyo, Fritz. 2015. AP Has a Robot Journalist that Writes a Thousand Articles per Month. *Tech Times*, October 10. http://www.techtimes.com/articles/93473/20151010/ap-has-a-robot-journalist-that-writes-a-thousand-articles-per-month.htm

Lanier, Jaron. 2010. *You Are Not a Gadget*. New York: Knopf Doubleday.

Miller, Jennifer. 2016. A New Dimension in Home Buying: Virtual Reality. *New York Times,* February 12, Real Estate Sec. http://www.nytimes.com/2016/02/14/realestate/virtual-reality-to-sell-homes.html

Paine, Thomas. 1797; reprint 1824. Agrarian Justice. In *The Political Writings of Thomas Paine,* 404–405. 2 vols. Charlestown: George Davidson.

Powell, Devin. 2015. A Flexible Circuit Has Been Injected into Living Brains. *Smithsonian.com*, June 8. http://www.smithsonianmag.com/science-nature/flexible-circuit-has-been-injected-living-brains-180955525/#eKhTIO9rPqHc6Urv.99

Prodhan, Georgina. 2016. Europe's Robots to Become 'Electronic Persons' Under Draft Plan. *Reuters,* June 21. http://www.reuters.com/article/us-europe-robotics-lawmaking-idUSKCN0Z72AY

Sanchez Diez, Maria. 2015. The Dutch 'Basic Income' Experiment Is Expanding Across Multiple Cities. *Quartz,* August 13. http://qz.com/473779/several-dutch-cities-want-to-give-residents-a-no-strings-attached-basic-income/

Sirkin, Harold L., Michael Zinser, and Justin Rose. 2015. Why Advanced Manufacturing Will Boost Productivity. *Boston Consulting Group*, January 30. https://www.bcgperspectives.com/content/articles/lean_and_manufacturing_production_why_advanced_manufacturing_boost_productivity/

Speight, Janek. 2015. Aussie Brick-Laying Robot Works 20 Times Faster than Humans. *Techly,* July 23. http://www.techly.com.au/2015/07/23/aussie-bricklaying-robot-works-20-times-faster-humans/

Un, Sushma. 2016a. Fewer Americans Can Afford Housing Despite Improvement in the Overall Market. *Marketwatch,* June 24. http://www.marketwatch.com/story/fewer-americans-can-afford-housing-despite-improvement-in-the-overall-market-2016-06-24

———. 2016b. World's First 'Robot Run' Farm to Open in Japan. *Phys.org*, February 1. http://phys.org/news/2016-02-world-robot-farm-japan.html

CHAPTER 2

Is Technological Unemployment Real?
An Assessment and a Plea for Abundance
Economics

Melanie Swan

INTRODUCTION

A persistent contemporary economic worry is technological unemployment (job loss due to automation). In some sense, technological unemployment is a thinkability problem similar to global warming: political incentives are packaged in shorter time frames than are appropriate for tackling the problem. Here, I suggest a larger frame of conceptualization that sees technological unemployment as a partial inevitability that some economies are already addressing with comprehensive solutions. In general, my view takes on the challenge, if not fully the optimism, of President John F. Kennedy's remark in 1962 that "if people have the talent to invent new machines that put people out of work, then they have the talent to put those people back to work" (Thompson 2015). Specifically, I argue that a new philosophy of economics, *Abundance Economics*, is necessary for the contemporary moment, and that the most successful economies of the future will understand economics as a way to manage the production and consumption of social goods in addition to material goods. In Part I of this chapter, I discuss the theme

M. Swan (✉)
New School for Social Research, New York, NY, USA
e-mail: m@melanieswan.com

© The Author(s) 2017   19
K. LaGrandeur, J.J. Hughes (eds.), *Surviving the Machine Age*,
DOI 10.1007/978-3-319-51165-8_2

of "the future of work" and address technological unemployment, jobless growth, and income inequality. In Part II, I describe Abundance Economics as an economic theory of the future.

PART I: THE PROBLEM: TECHNOLOGICAL UNEMPLOYMENT, INCOME INEQUALITY, AND THE AUTOMATION ECONOMY

The Nature of Technological Unemployment

On the one hand, technological unemployment is the dream and apogee of humans' achievement in the world. Arthur C. Clarke, in his literary depiction of the human future, has noted that "the goal of the future is full unemployment" (Kreider 2012). Likewise, as far back as the 1930s, economist John Maynard Keynes envisioned a 15-hour work week, because he thought that the economies of our time would outrun the need for labor faster than we could find new uses for it, and he also predicted a society in which the accumulation of wealth would no longer be of high social importance (Keynes 1963). However, while technological unemployment seems to have arrived, it does not appear to be utopian, because one of its results is uneven economic consequences. The problem is that those who become unemployed by technology are not being reabsorbed or planned for comprehensively in today's society. A broader, systems-level approach to technological unemployment, such as the one that includes efforts to train and direct individuals toward the jobs of the future and to coordinate planning activities between business, governmental, and educational entities, would be more effective than the haphazard approach we currently have. This could help facilitate the smooth trajectories of the arrival of technological unemployment, as opposed to its current arrival in haphazard bursts with unintended consequences.

To grasp the current size, magnitude, and pace of technological unemployment, several studies and publications provide guidance. Overall, they make the case that technological unemployment could have a significant near-term impact, primarily one in which the gains could outweigh the costs, particularly if society were to influence outcomes with policy incentives and job-retraining programs. Studies confirm that faster technological progress may increase unemployment, at least during a transition period (Feldmann 2013, 1099). One analysis estimates that nearly half (47%) of all US employment is at risk of being automated in the next two decades, and lists 702 jobs that could be impacted (Frey and

Osborne 2013, 44). By extension, this could apply to many other countries worldwide. A report from the World Economic Forum highlights the trend of the overall net loss of jobs: 5.1 million global jobs lost in the period 2015–2020 (WEF 2016, 1). Other examinations offer a different view: for example, wondering why there are still so many jobs in a world that could be automating more quickly (Autor 2015).

The Pew Research Center presents a balanced stance, discussing both the benefits and the detriments of technological unemployment (Smith and Anderson 2014, 5). Some of the potential benefits are that technological advances have always been a net creator of jobs, including in situations of high-magnitude change. Even if jobs are displaced in the short-term, this job loss could be seen in the context of longer economic time cycles that ultimately result in growth. Humans are good at adapting to new situations, and this includes inventing new types of work to adapt to changing economic circumstances. The central point is that technology is continuing to deliver on its promise to free humans from drudgery, and it is up to us to organize society around this fact. Further, technological unemployment is already starting to produce the social good of defining "work" in a more positive and socially beneficial way—as productive human effort instead of sustenance labor.

On the other hand, some of the potential costs of technological unemployment result from its disproportionate impact on society. One example of this is the bifurcation of the labor force: highly skilled workers in certain industries are better poised to succeed, while others are being displaced into lower-paying service industry jobs or into a state of permanent unemployment. Also, blue-collar employment is being impacted more than white-collar employment, and women more than men (Brinded 2016). Pew Research further notes that the educational system is inadequate for future work preparation, a topic addressed in more detail by David Gunkel in another chapter of this book.

Jobless Growth

Technological unemployment cannot be evaluated as a standalone phenomenon since productivity, jobs, and economic growth are highly interrelated. The main economic question is whether technological unemployment is a "new" situation or not. Are there structural changes to the economy, or is today's technological unemployment part of persistent long-term trend, albeit one that we have not recognized? While it is unclear if the current moment of technological unemployment is a symptom of a structural change or instead merely the continuation of a long-term trend, the situation of jobless growth at present does seem clear. In the wake of the 2008 financial crisis, gains have been seen in most measures of economic health, particularly productivity; however, there has not been a corresponding growth in jobs. One study points to evidence of jobless growth by indicating that unemployment increased by more than 5.7% between May 2007, and October 2009, simultaneous with increases in automation (Brynjolfsson and McAfee 2011). Another study finds that 44% of companies that have cut down on employees since 2008 did so by replacing their functions with automation (McKinsey 2011). These examples suggest that technological unemployment could be one explanation for the recent jobless growth. This could persist because capital, in the form of technology, is being effectively substituted for labor (*The Economist* 2014).

The fact that the nature of technological unemployment is changing could also influence the velocity and reach of the substitution of technology for labor. Automation is no longer being confined to routine tasks, since machine learning algorithms, cloud-based big data, and predictive analytics are quickly enabling new kinds of technology applications. Self-driving vehicles are one example of how technology is assuming more complicated tasks. Commercial driving is anticipated to be one of the next sectors of labor to be automated (Nuwer 2015). By one estimate, long-distance truck driving in the USA could be fully automated by 2025 (Collins 2015). The complexities of commercial driving require a second order of innovation in the form of vehicle-to-vehicle communication networks to coordinate autonomous vehicles. In addition to driving, other sectors to see greater degrees of automation and technological unemployment in the immediate future could include manufacturing, distribution and logistics, administrative functions, and financial and legal services (WEF 2016, 3; Croft 2016).

The current situation of technological unemployment can be better understood by considering some analogous economic examples. One such example is outsourcing, where, over the past several decades, a significant number of jobs have shifted to countries with more efficient cost profiles. There were fears of job loss, but the worldwide economy eventually adjusted to the situation. Indeed, in one sense, technological unemployment can be seen as a continuation of outsourcing in the sense that it arises from online outsourcing and technological outsourcing. The same diversity of arguments as to whether outsourcing's overall impact has been favorable or detrimental would apply to technological outsourcing. One lesson could be that adjustment takes time on the order of years or decades but eventually occurs, and that it is a combination of structural change and the continuation of long-term trends.

An illustration of this is the industrial revolution. Similar to the current case of automation, there were diverse approaches to the industrial revolution. Some countries quickly embraced the new technologies (UK, Belgium), while others (France) had a more measured implementation. In some sense, both the industrial revolution and outsourcing are examples of the more general case of adopting any new technology. The best program could be one of *smart adoption*, as opposed to forced adoption or fearful non-adoption. Smart adoption in the case of technological unemployment suggests a long-term, multi-sector economic planning effort. A change on the order of the industrial revolution took 50–100 years to fully propagate through worldwide nation-state economies. Therefore, it is difficult to make statements regarding technological unemployment because it is a recent situation that has arisen most clearly since 2008. If technological unemployment is a significant macro-level structural change to the economy, longer time frames will be needed to fully assess its impact. Further, any complex economic situation is difficult to gauge while in progress. The example above regarding the industrial revolution also underlines that while dramatic economic changes eventually have a universal impact, the benefits accrue unevenly.

Overall, technological unemployment and jobless growth could be long-term trends that precipitate structural economic change. Irrespective of measurability challenges, they should be addressed, particularly through macro-economic policy. A related issue highlighted by technological unemployment, for which there might be better, targeted interventions, is income inequality.

Income Inequality

Income inequality refers to the uneven distribution of income within a society, and a case can be made that it is a worsening global problem that has both economic and social consequences. An Organization for Economic Cooperation and Development report finds that "in OECD countries, the richest 10% of the population earn 9.6 times the income of the poorest 10%" (DeSilver 2015). Another study claims that the world's wealthiest 0.1% of individuals control a concentrated portion of income, the size of which has not been seen since before World War I (Piketty 2014). In countries such as the USA and the UK, corporate top-to-bottom pay ratios are routinely 300:1 for the CEO as compared with the lowest-paid worker (Anderson 2015; Wilkinson and Pickett 2014). In the USA, the Census Bureau reports that "the top 5% of households received 21.8% of income in 2014, while the bottom 60% received 27.1%" (DeSilver 2015). Further, the American middle class has been shrinking. In 2015, after more than four decades of being the nation's economic majority, the middle class was overtaken in number by those in other economic tiers (120.8 million adults in middle-income households as compared with 121.3 million in lower- and upper-income households combined) (Fry and Kochhar 2015).

A related phenomenon is that income inequality is not an isolated problem but has widespread negative effects on the whole of society. One study finds that all social problems are more common in less equal societies. These include violence, mental illness, drug addiction, obesity, imprisonment, and poorer social conditions for children. Health and social problems were found to be two to ten times more prevalent in societies with greater income inequality (Wilkinson and Pickett 2014). In the case of mental illness, income rank was seen as a better predictor of developing an illness than absolute income. Other studies found effects on stress, cognitive performance, and emotional well-being: for example, links between income inequality and child maltreatment and bullying (Eckenrode 2014; Due 2009). Other examinations documented the literal "pollution effect" of income inequality on health outcomes (Subramanian and Kawachi 2004). Further, the social costs of income inequality were found to be endemic, persisting across all countries, states, and provinces: for example, the more equal provinces of China tend to fare better than the less equal ones (Wilkinson and Pickett 2014). This evidence supports the case that income inequality exists, is worsening, and has significant social effects beyond the economic domain.

The important question, then, is how we can resolve this problem and its attendant social consequences. In terms of policy, how do we balance the promotion of income inequality with the social costs of doing so? Even if some countries wanted to make improvements to income inequality, the degree to which it might actually be possible could be problematic, given country ideology, size, and diversity. For example, such policies might be more readily deployable in smaller countries with greater homogeneity in values, and thus the cohesion and trust necessary for implementation. In other cases, the sheer size and diversity of a country could be a challenge. The USA is many times the size of some countries with greater income equality, for example, such as Denmark, and does not have as homogeneous a population as that country does. Also, in some sense, income inequality is an example of a "first-world" problem, in that only wealthy societies are equipped to identify and address it. Moreover, cultural attitudes may stand in the way of resolving income inequality: given the value systems of certain countries such the USA, where capitalism is the norm, income inequality seems more likely to persist there than in other countries such as Scandinavia, where socialist economics is more accepted and where income inequality reduction has already been a long-term policy objective.

PART II: THE SOLUTION: A NEW PHILOSOPHY OF ECONOMIC THEORY

To address the long-term structural effects of automation as outlined in Part I, one foundational resource that might be helpful is a new overall philosophy of economic theory, and as such I propose *Abundance Economics*. The challenges of automation arise from outdated and monolithic economic principles. Increasingly, traditional economic notions of material scarcity are no longer valid in today's digital economies. Traditional premises of economic theory will prove even less tenable as the automation economy progresses.

The cornerstone of most economic theory has been the idea of scarcity. Traditionally conceived, economic systems are those engaged in the production and distribution of scarce material goods. However, there are existing and emerging situations in the world where scarcity is not a parameter, or in any case not the governing parameter. For example, with electronic goods such as software and digital images, there is essentially no cost to marginal production: the production and distribution of an additional unit is simply done by copying and sending the goods electronically (Rifkin 2015). There is no additional cost to one person or one million people listening to a song. Additionally, a broad share of the goods valorized in the contemporary economy is intangible. These include non-monetary currencies such as reputation, intention, attention, access, influence, choice, autonomy, recognition, and creativity. Intangible goods have properties that are different from material goods; they are often complementary and non-rival, and they can make more of themselves when consumed (in economic terms, they can agglomerate). Thus, a new philosophy of economic theory is needed to make sense of digital economics.

One first step in articulating a new philosophy of economic theory that more appropriately corresponds to the automation economy is setting forth some mind-set shifts: from *labor to fulfillment, scarcity to abundance*, and *hierarchy to decentralization*. The first principle, transitioning from *labor to fulfillment*, means reorienting our thinking from a labor-based economy to a fulfillment-based economy. The second principle, shifting from *scarcity to abundance*, means seeing the world's resources in a paradigm of availability as opposed to paucity. The third principle, moving from notions of *hierarchy to decentralization*, means apprehending that modes of organization may be centralized or decentralized (or both), where decentralization may be better in certain cases, particularly for very large-scale endeavors. The first two relate most to the situation of automation and technological unemployment.

The most immediate concept to revamp is scarcity, specifically the presumption of scarcity as the core precept of most economic systems. Even scarcity's opposite, abundance, is an impoverished formulation as currently conceived. This is because abundance is primarily understood quantitatively to be the zero-sum alleviation of scarcity, which it is, but it is also more (see Fig. 2.1). In the first sense, abundance is the eradication of scarcity in terms of having material needs met, recouping a quantitative baseline for survival. In the second sense, abundance is also an important upside formulation concerning the quality of life. Abundance means a qualitative sense

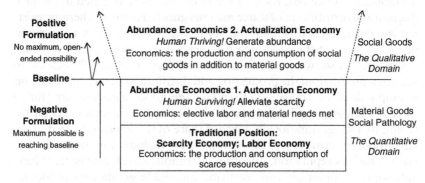

Fig. 2.1 Abundance Economics

Population growth

of open-ended possibility, boundless improvement trajectories up from the baseline metric into new territory. Abundance starts to attend to the social goods that humans need to thrive, those goods that pertain to their quality of life, not merely the material goods they need to survive.

Social goods traditionally mean goods or services that benefit all persons in a society, for example, clean air, clean water, electricity, literacy, and Wi-Fi. Here I extend the term to mean quality-of-life social goods such as autonomy, recognition, and trust. Other important social goods include agency, mutuality, respect, acknowledgment, contribution, collaboration, creativity, participation, and belonging. For example, societies with a higher level of trust (a direct result of better income equality) have been able to modernize more quickly and remain more globally competitive than others (e.g., in the digitization of health, finance, banking, and payment systems).

While material goods enable survival, social goods enable thriving. Abundance Economics is concerned with both. Scarcity creates negative social goods, or social pathologies, such as income inequality. Addressing potential technological unemployment from a policy perspective can help to reduce negative social goods, including "technological anxiety" (Mokyr et al.,2015), and uncertainty about the effects of automation. Whereas the *Scarcity Economy* is a fixed-pie, zero-sum game and focuses directly or indirectly on creating social pathologies, the *Abundance Economy* is an expanding-pie model with open-ended possibility.

There are two phases for achieving Abundance Economics. The first step is an eradication of material-goods scarcity by way of the automation economy, recouping a baseline ideal. The second step is the creation of social goods through the actualization economy. The automation economy, if well-executed, can help in the first phase to meet the survival needs of all people. However, to truly extend human quality of life beyond sustenance, the open-ended formulation of abundance as the production and consumption of social goods is needed. The bigger issue is attending to quality of life, not merely the impact of automation.

Abundance Economics Phase I: Automation Economy Alleviates Material-Goods Scarcity

The automation economy comprises the phase of Abundance Economics that alleviates scarcity and reaches a baseline of material-goods sustenance. It is one in which technology has supplemented or replaced non-elective human labor. Presumably, labor-based "work" would not fully disappear, but could be executed out of choice as opposed to necessity. In the labor-to-fulfillment mind-set shift, work becomes a concept of optional productive engagement for the purpose of personal fulfillment, not a sustenance requirement. Decoupling labor-based work from sustenance-remuneration is an idea different countries are exploring. One proposal is to institute programs such as guaranteed basic income (GBI) initiatives, paying individuals a monthly basic income to cover survival needs, a concept discussed in a number of other chapters in the present collection of essays. Some universal or GBI pilot programs are being tested in Europe and in Canada. The test-cases are both a forward-looking experiment for bringing about a smooth transition to the automation economy, and a practical response to the inefficiencies of welfare systems. The electorate has not so much resisted the essential concept of GBI programs as much as the possibility it might increase immigration—which only serves to confirm their perceived value (Foulkes 2016).

A new form of jobs, "jobs of the future," could be necessary to produce and maintain the future economy. There might be many fulfilling and remunerative employment categories of the future. Some possible examples we could imagine based on current developments are neuro-implant technician, urban farmer, virtual reality experience designer, 3D printing specialist, smart-home handyperson, remote health care specialist, and freelance professor (Grothaus 2015). Other jobs of the future could include blockchain smart-contract writers, audio interface designers, and social robotics interaction specialists (Swan 2015). While the need for labor work requiring human expertise and ingenuity might not go away, it could be reshaped to offer a wider range of participation and compensation choices to individuals. The economy is already configuring demand for some of these job categories of the future. Entrepreneurs could target the productive fulfillment market directly, by designing jobs of the future that offer intrinsic meaning and fulfillment.

Abundance Economics Phase II: Actualization Economy Creates Social Goods for Human Thriving

Whereas jobs of the future (elective work, possibly with augmented incentives) are needed to achieve a new form of economy based on self-fulfillment, "lives of the future" are needed to achieve the second phase of Abundance Economics, the actualization economy. The *actualization economy* more fully incorporates the mind-set shift from labor to fulfillment, wherein humans are thriving, not merely surviving. Articulating lives of the future exposes our impoverished concept of work, and our division of life into work and leisure. Beyond the work–leisure binary of the labor economy, there could be many different categories of life activities such as life-long learning, unpaid vocations (teaching, mentoring, coaching, leading, facilitating), health and sports (movement, exercise, team and league participations), creative expression (art, music, singing), community participations (civic, political), collaboration (engaging with others on projects or goals), interaction (friends, family, acquaintances, associates), spiritual and mindfulness activities, and entertainment (relaxation, play, fun, discovery). Beyond work for pay, these opportunities for meaningful engagement could create as much work as needed, and produce many valuable social goods.

In the contemporary labor economy, what seems to account for the "good life" is the idea of some sort of work–life balance, but in Abundance Economics the definition is much broader. The good life expands to a fuller multi-category experience of life in which self-directed agents produce and consume social goods, and in which labor–work no longer centrally defines human existence. Thus, with an orientation to both social and material goods production, Abundance Economics is a model for generating an improved quality of life that goes beyond sustenance needs.

Discussion and Limitations

There are many potential limitations to the Abundance Economics proposed here. Abundance Economics might be overly optimistic and unrealistic to achieve. It would be nice to foster the growth of social goods, but precisely how to accomplish this in practice is not clear. One problem is that qualitative measurement metrics are not yet fully established, despite some promising emerging methods such as "cliodynamics" (Turchin 2005).

Measurement is difficult, but a more intractable challenge is social incentives. It may be that political hierarchies will have little reason to adopt policies supporting social goods production if there is a risk of eroding their power base. Social goods can be generated by other means such as crowdsourcing, but this has proved difficult so far (Murray 2015). Hierarchical social organization presents further challenges because the current structure of the ownership of the means of production is likely to persist. At present, the funders of new technology still become the owners of new technology, and accrue wealth and influence from this, and that, in turn, contributes to income inequality. The present power structure is likely to continue unless alternative models of the ownership of the means of production are implemented. While there might be less of a requirement for physical plant means-of-production in the digital era, we could nevertheless expect that new forms of influence and control that favor existing hierarchies would be similarly instantiated in the automation and actualization economy.

Further, perhaps one of the most intransigent limitations to future change is complacency. Depending upon the level of remuneration built into potential GBI initiatives, there might be little incentive for anyone to be interested in the production of any goods, whether social or material. In fact, arguably, complacency is already a social good (or social pathology) produced by many economies, even if mostly as an unintended consequence. However, the hopeful view is that the human drive to apply energy productively and enjoyably toward challenge and meaning will persist. As discussed, the entrepreneurial call to action is precisely to design the *experiences of the future* that cater to meaningful engagement of productive energy and improved quality of life.

CONCLUSION

In this chapter, I proposed a new philosophy of economic theory, *Abundance Economics*, to address the contemporary moment of technological automation and technological unemployment. Automation and its effects are likely to persist as crucial economic drivers. Abundance Economics appropriates automation by rethinking the traditional economic principles of scarce resource distribution in two phases. First, there is an alleviation of quantitative material-goods scarcity in the automation economy to support human survival needs. Second, there is the creation of qualitative social goods in the actualization economy to enable human thriving. I suggest that the most successful future economies will be those that enact economics as systems for the production and consumption of social goods in addition to material goods. Such an emphasis on social goods that improve human quality of life could be crucial in helping to transition to a potential situation of rapid automation across multiple sectors of the economy.

Overall, automation and technological unemployment should be a substantial long-term positive gain for the worldwide economy. The key challenge is to implement these structural changes in ways that benefit all persons. There is no economic law that producing a good or service must require human labor (Huff 2015), and we should not limit our imagination to projects achievable only by human labor. Instead, we can be thinking about much larger, Kardashev-level (i.e., planetary) projects that might be possible through automation, such as large-scale environmental cleanup, agricultural monitoring, and space settlement. These are the abundant futures toward which Clarke and Keynes both gestured.

References

Anderson, Sarah. 2015. This Is Why Your CEO Makes More Than 300 Times Your Pay. *Fortune*, August 7. http://fortune.com/2015/08/07/ceo-pay-ratio-sec-income-inequality/

Autor, David. 2015. Why Are There Still So Many Jobs? The History and Future of Workplace Automation. *Journal of Economic Perspectives* 29(3): 3–30.

Brinded, Lianna. 2016. Women Are Going to Lose Out the Most When Robots Take Over the World's Workforce. *Business Insider*, January 18. http://www.businessinsider.com/wef-tech-industrial-revolution-report-women-lose-the-most-jobs-2016-1

Brynjolfsson, Erik, and Andrew McAfee. 2011. Technology's Influence on Employment and the Economy. In *Race Against the Machine*. Cambridge, MA: Digital Frontier Press.

Croft, Jane. 2016. More than 100,000 Legal Roles to Become Automated. *Financial Times, March 15.* https://www.ft.com/content/c8ef3f62-ea9c-11e5-888e-2eadd5fbc4a4

Collins, Andrew P. 2015. Autonomous Driving Long-Distance Trucks Will Be a Reality in Ten Years. *TruckYeah!*, July 11. http://truckyeah.jalopnik.com/autonomous-driving-long-distance-trucks-will-be-a-reali-1603746933
Croft, Jane. "More than 100,000 legal roles to become automated." *Financial Times*, 2016.

DeSilver, Drew. 2015. The Many Ways to Measure Economic Inequality. *Pew Research Center*, September 22. http://www.pewresearch.org/fact-tank/2015/09/22/the-many-ways-to-measure-economic-inequality/

Due, Pernille, Juan Merlo, Yossi Harel-Fisch, et al. 2009. Socioeconomic Inequality in Exposure to Bullying During Adolescence: A Comparative, Cross-Sectional, Multilevel Study in 35 Countries. *American Journal of Public Health* 99 (5): 907–914.

Eckenrode, John, Elliott G. Smith, Margaret E. McCarthy, and Michael Dineen. 2014. Income Inequality and Child Maltreatment in the United States. *Pediatrics* 133 (3): 454–461.

Feldmann, Horst. 2013. Technological Unemployment in Industrial Countries. *Journal of Evolutionary Economics* 23(5): 1099–1126.

Foulkes, Imogen. 2016. Switzerland Basic Income: Landmark Vote Looms. *BBC News*, June 4. http://www.bbc.com/news/world-europe-36443512

Frey, Carl, and Michael Osborne. 2013. The Future of Employment: How Susceptible Are Jobs to Computerisation? *Oxford University*, September 17. http://www.oxfordmartin.ox.ac.uk/downloads/academic/The_Future_of_Employment.pdf

Fry, Richard, and Rakesh Kochhar. 2015. The American Middle Class Is Losing Ground. *Pew Research Center*, December 10. http://www.pewresearch.org/fact-tank/2015/12/10/5-takeaways-about-the-american-middle-class/

Grothaus, Michael. 2015. The Top Jobs in 10 Years Might Not Be What You Expect. *Fast Company*, May 18. http://www.fastcompany.com/3046277/the-new-rules-of-work/the-top-jobs-in-10-years-might-not-be-what-you-expect

Huff, Gerald. 2015. The Labor Content Fallacy. *Medium*, August 25. https://medium.com/@geraldhuff/the-labor-content-fallacy-96b8ddadf5cd#.9vd0rhod1

Keynes, John M. 1963. Economic Possibilities for Our Grandchildren. In *Essays in Persuasion*, 358–373. New York: WW Norton & Co.

Kreider, Tim. 2012. The 'Busy' Trap. *New York Times*, June 30. http://opinionator.blogs.nytimes.com/2012/06/30/the-busy-trap/?_r=0

McKinsey Global Institute. 2011. *An Economy that Works: Job Creation and America's Future*. New York: McKinsey and Co.http://www.mckinsey.com/global-themes/employment-and-growth/an-economy-that-works-for-us-job-creation

Mokyr, Joel, Chris Vickers, and Nicolas L. Ziebarth. 2015. The History of Technological Anxiety and the Future of Economic Growth: Is This Time Different? *Journal of Economic Perspectives* 29(3): 31–50.

Murray, Charles. 2015. *By the People: Rebuilding Liberty Without Permission*. New York: Crown Forum.

Nuwer, Rachel. 2015. Will Machines Eventually Take on Every Job? *BBC News*, August 6. http://www.bbc.com/future/story/20150805-will-machines-eventually-take-on-every-job

Piketty, Thomas. 2014. *Capital in the Twenty-First Century*. Cambridge, MA: Belknap Press.

———. 2015. *The Zero Marginal Cost Society: The Internet of Things, the Collaborative Commons, and the Eclipse of Capitalism*. New York: St. Martin's Griffin.

Smith, Aaron and Janna Anderson. 2014. AI, Robotics, and the Future of Jobs. *Pew Research Center*, August 6. http://www.pewinternet.org/2014/08/06/future-of-jobs/

Subramanian, S.V., and Ichiro Kawachi. 2004. Income Inequality and Health: What Have We Learned So Far? *Epidemiologic Reviews* 26 (1): 78–91.

Swan, Melanie. 2015. *Blockchain: Blueprint for a New Economy.* Sebastopol: O'Reilly Media.

The Economist. 2014. The Onrushing Wave: Previous Technological Innovation has Always Delivered More Long-run Employment, Not Less. But Things Can Change. *The Economist.*

Thompson, Derek. 2015. A World Without Work. *The Atlantic, July/August.* https://www.theatlantic.com/magazine/archive/2015/07/world-without-work/395294/

Turchin, Peter. 2005. *War and Peace and War: The Life Cycles of Imperial Nations.* New York: Pi Press.

Wilkinson, Richard and Kate Pickett. 2014. The Spirit Level Authors: Why Society Is More Unequal Than Ever. *The Guardian*, March 9. https://www.theguardian.com/commentisfree/2014/mar/09/society-unequal-the-spirit-level

World Economic Forum (WEF). 2016. *The Future of Jobs: Employment, Skills and Workforce Strategy for the Fourth Industrial Revolution*, January. http://www3.weforum.org/docs/WEF_Future_of_Jobs.pdf

Creative Destruction: Emerging Technology and the Changing Course of Job Creation

James P. Clark

CREATIVE DESTRUCTION

Many economists and certainly most capitalists have embraced that term since Joseph Schumpeter first used it in 1942 in the phrase "the perennial gale of creative destruction" in *Capitalism, Socialism, and Democracy* (82). The idea is that the growth in a capitalist economy comes from the stormy turnover due to innovation or what Schumpeter called "industrial mutation"(83) and that even though it causes disruptions and loss of jobs, it's all worth it due to the growth that results. He said it was "the essential fact about capitalism" (83), and most economists since would characterize it as the best description of the evolution of economies over the past few centuries, particularly since the start of the industrial revolution. In 1930—a year when, of course, unemployment was on everyone's mind—John Maynard Keynes, in an essay entitled "Economic Possibilities for our Grandchildren," imagined a new "disease" which he called "technological

---

This essay is adapted from keynote address given at The World Summit on Technological Unemployment, convened by the World Technology Network, September 29, 2015, TIME Inc. Conference Center, New York City.

J.P. Clark (✉)
World Technology Network (WTN.net), New York, NY, USA
e-mail: jpclark@wtn.net

K. LaGrandeur, J.J. Hughes (eds.), *Surviving the Machine Age*,
DOI 10.1007/978-3-319-51165-8_3

unemployment." The crux of this disease, he said, was the possibility that "due to our discovery of means of economising the use of labour we may outrun the pace at which we can find new uses for labour" (325). In this chapter, I will go into more depth on these topics and related issues, most particularly examining if there is something fundamentally different about our era.

The Historical Observation

In the "Concise Encyclopedia of Economics," W. Michael Cox and Richard Alm write that

> Schumpeter and the economists who adopt his succinct summary of the free market's ceaseless churning echo capitalism's critics in acknowledging that lost jobs, ruined companies, and vanishing industries are inherent parts of the growth system. The saving grace comes from recognizing the good that comes from the turmoil. Over time, societies that allow creative destruction to operate grow more productive and richer; their citizens see the benefits of new and better products, shorter work weeks, better jobs, and higher living standards. Herein lies the paradox of progress.... Schumpeter's enduring term reminds us that capitalism's pain and gain are inextricably linked. The process of creating new industries does not go forward without sweeping away the preexisting order. (2007)

As Cox and Alm further point out in that same article, in 1900, there were 109,000 horse carriage and harness makers in the United States, and in 1910, a total of 238,000 people worked as blacksmiths. However, the new technological innovation of the automobile erased virtually all of those jobs and replaced them with many more jobs in much larger industries in the decades that followed. And that phenomenon of job destruction that creates yet more new jobs has been the historical trend in all previous industrial revolutions.

A recent award-winning study (2015) by economists Ian Stewart, Debapratim De, and Alex Cole at the consulting firm Deloitte looked at English census data starting from 1871. Their conclusion was that technology is not only a great job-creating machine, but because the new jobs increase overall spending power, that itself creates new demand and new jobs. They also point out that the job-destroying effects of technological change are easier to notice than the creative side of the phenomenon.

As a result, capitalists have been willing to tolerate and usually even unreservedly champion creative destruction in economics because the historical observation has been that it creates more net new jobs than it destroys.

THE SUFFERING AND THE THEORY

The crucial problem is that it has also been historically observed that the people who lose their jobs due to technological innovation are not usually the same ones who get the new types of jobs, and the resulting suffering can, as we know, be immense.

One cannot discuss these issues without referring to the Luddites, the legendary English textile workers who rebelled in the period from around 1811 to 1816, when their jobs were threatened by new labor-saving weaving technologies which appeared in those early decades of the Industrial Revolution powered by steam. They weren't just mildly protesting: in the end, a massive military force was required to put down the movement, which ranged across most of Northwestern England. If this has happened before, it can happen again.

As the Industrial Revolution (note that it wasn't called the Industrial "Evolution," given the incredible gale of creative destruction) spread across Europe in the nineteenth century, generating huge urban influxes, new forms of employment in new industries, and massive waves of unemployment in response to a barely adjusting roller-coaster economy, we unsurprisingly witnessed new theories of labor and employment emerging as well. Most famously and significantly, Karl Marx delved deep into the underpinnings, incentives, and contradictions inherent in the latest phase of capitalism.

His theory of unemployment, stated in *Capital*, was that, "The whole form of the movement of modern industry depends...upon the constant transformation of a part of the labouring population into unemployed or half employed hands" (1936, 694–695). Much as did the conservative economists a century later, he argued that unemployment is built into the capitalist economy and that periods of mass unemployment are to be expected regularly. The surplus labor fights for scarce jobs, thereby keeping wages low (and profits high), and pitting job seekers against each other in an environment of economic anxiety. Interestingly, in addition to the previously mentioned theory of unemployment, Marx also discusses the Luddites in *Capital*, where he says, "The instrument of labour, when it takes the form of a machine, immediately becomes a competitor of the workman himself" (470).

But it doesn't take only Marx or a Marxist to theorize compellingly about unemployment. In traditional economics, "structural unemployment" has to do with a gap between who wants a job and the skills required for the open jobs. Given the lag time it takes for a new entrant to the workforce to acquire the skills necessary, or to un-learn old skills and relearn the new ones, we can easily imagine how issues of structural employment have also been core-level contributions to the problem of technological unemployment over the past few centuries. And one can also easily imagine how a period of rapid technological innovation such as our own would bring such issues even more to the fore. If the technologies being adopted now are designed to replace humans entirely with machines and software to do the same or new jobs, the option of a human worker's learning new skills for jobs that humans won't be doing becomes, of course, a moot point.

Unemployment may on one level be a dry academic study of what happens to surplus labor in an economy, but for those experiencing it, it is an all-too-real and likely severely negative period of life. Unemployment means that often, of course, one runs out of money and cannot pay one's bills or debts. It may even mean the inability to maintain shelter, and so it is often a primary cause of homelessness. Unemployment causes health problems, both physical and psychological. It has been shown to increase susceptibility to anxiety, depression, and heart disease, and tracks with increased crime, spousal abuse, and alcohol, tobacco, and drug use, as well as poor diet, and even suicide...not to mention divorce and family breakup (Meade et al. 2013). And the ripple effects of all of these issues are as innumerable as the social, financial, and mental health problems that impact humans in the modern world.

THE POLITICAL DANGERS

On the political level, of course, high levels of unemployment (or even pervasive economic anxiety around the prospect of job loss) have proven to be one of the most dangerous triggers of political instability and subsequent demagoguery on both the left and the right. One can usually see xenophobia or anti-immigrant sentiment coinciding with periods of high unemployment or economic anxiety. It's a lot easier to blame a foreigner or recent immigrant than it is to blame the less visible macro-economic forces such as technologically driven industrial change. Totalitarianism and/or fascism (or at least way stations along the path) have also evolved out of periods of high economic anxiety and unemployment. In just one of many examples, when Hitler came to power, following the fall of the Weimer Republic in 1933, no one would argue that the high unemployment rate of over 20%—in one of the most industrialized/technological innovation-driven nations in the world at that time—didn't play a key role.

Elected governments (and even unelected ones) have usually risen and fallen during and around extended or deep periods of unemployment, or at the very least because of how they appear to deal with it. And the politicians (and those who are the primary guardians of capitalism) know it. Politicians, political parties, and, in many cases, revolutionaries seek to position themselves in order to capitalize (no pun intended) on the disruption or on the proposed solution. One could argue, in some sense, that the history of the modern world—say since the industrial revolution over three centuries ago—is the history of creative destruction...or, to put it another way, the history of the modern world is the history of technological unemployment.

THE FUTURE

There's a divide right now in the debate between what one could call the techno-optimists and the techno-pessimists. Many of the so-called techno-optimists and the vast majority of capitalists argue that creative destruction due to technological innovation will continue to play out positively in the coming years and perhaps even without much of a hitch. The most intense techno-pessimists think we are headed for a job-pocalypse that will unravel civilization and that there is no way to avoid it. Where you stand on the immense historical drama that has begun to unfold will likely determine how you choose to respond to it.

To give some context on where I stand and to what I am about to argue regarding this issue, let me give some personal background. I am the founder and chairman of the World Technology Network. The WTN—as many call it—is a global community of the peer-elected most innovative people and organizations in science and technology and related fields. We give out the annual World Technology Awards in 20 different categories, including not only the sci-tech fields of IT-Hardware, Software, Communications Technology, Biotech, Health, Energy, Materials, and Space, but also fields such as the Arts, Design, Ethics, Education, Environment, Policy, and many more. The winners and finalists of the Awards became our Fellows, and we now have over 1000 Fellows spread out over 40 countries. They are elected by their peers for doing work of the greatest likely long-term significance. We presented the Awards in a ceremony at the end of our annual World Technology Summit.

We also convene more focused events. And most relevantly, in September 2015, at TIME Inc. headquarters, we convened the World Summit on Technological Unemployment (WSTU). We brought together over 25 high-level experts for a packed day of exploration of the topic. Participants included President Clinton's former Labor Secretary, Robert Reich; President Obama's Treasury Secretary, Larry Summers; and Nobel Prize-winning economist, Joseph Stiglitz, among many others.

The WTN is truly in touch with those creating many of the actual innovations that are already or soon to disrupt virtually every industry and every aspect of civilization. I've been exposed to the information and the people that help me understand the trend lines of our current technological civilization, and my role with the WTN has allowed me to have more confidence as we sift through the core question we are facing here: When it comes to the process of creative destruction and its ability to generate more net new jobs than it destroys, is there something fundamentally different about our time?

Is There Something Fundamentally Different About Our Time?

Although we must respect the historical evidence that indicates that the process of creative destruction has caused a net growth in jobs in the past, it is at least conceivable to consider that now some new factors are at work and might more than marginally change the outcome going forward:

1. *In the past, technological innovation on a scale truly disruptive to an industry or a way of life occurred perhaps every few decades. People had more time to adjust.*

For most of human history, the pace of job-description change was so slow that a grandfather could be quite well assured that the job of his grandson would be remarkably similar to his own. Owing to the nature of what used to be called "women's work"—which was even less likely coupled to industrial innovation, from grandmother to granddaughter—this was likely even more true. When the Industrial Revolution hit, the grandson's job might be quite different from the grandfather's for the first time, and perhaps even from the father's. In both of those cases, there was theoretically enough lead time to allow for some sort of planned transition from one career or job-type to another to lessen the chances of unwanted unemployment driven by innovation in a given field. There was even time to engage in formal apprenticeship and/or training/education to prepare for a shift. We now live in an era where, due to the very nature of exponential technological change, there is simply no time for inter-generational scale preparation. In fact, a 4-year college degree is almost certainly out of date by the time a student graduates. Entire industries are shifting in their fundamentals every year or so. A person in an industry who neglects to keep up with news and trends for even a few months can feel woefully out of date these days.

2. *In the past, truly disruptive technological innovation did not occur in every industry at once. People could have more options to move to an un-disrupted industry.*

Think of the most significant innovations of all time. Think of the long but shrinking time gaps between the invention of fire, spoken language, farming, the ship, the wheel, money, written language, water power, the printing press, electricity, the engine, the light bulb, the telegraph, and the telephone. Think of the pace of innovation in the twentieth century. And think of the pace in recent years. A perceptive individual could (and did) navigate the shifting landscape of opportunity when a significant new innovation hit in the past and move from one disrupted industry to another. However, the point is that such disruptions didn't hit in the past at such an unrelentingly continual rate and in almost every industry at once. Again, people had much more time to adjust in order to avoid unemployment prompted by technological innovation.

3. *In the past, any economy built upon disruptive innovation was not fully globalized. People had more options to move to different parts of the world to find jobs in as-yet-undisrupted industries with which they were already familiar, and with good job prospects.*

Just as migration has been one of the dominant drivers of human history, technological innovation and the resulting economic displacement and unemployment have been primary drivers of migration. And, this migration was not just from one region of the world to another, or one country to another, but often simply from one region of a country to another. Technologically driven industrial change spread slowly until very recently in history.

We are now unarguably in a globalized economy. Globalization is a significant and contributive magnifier of the impact of technological innovation on employment. Innovations can create new industries and new jobs more quickly around the world, almost simultaneous with their penetration of their home market. But such innovations can also quickly destroy the pockets where the innovations in the past would have not so quickly reached, pockets which in the past would have provided refuge to those being displaced from their former home. In short, there is now nowhere in the globalized job market to escape the pace of technological change, nowhere to hide from it.

4. *In the past, most countries were growing in population, not aging and with a shrinking working-age population as is the case, for example, in Western Europe, Russia, and Japan now; this demographic trend puts even more pressure on non-human labor to make up the gap.*

Most of human history has been one of relatively flat population growth. It took until 1804 to reach 1 billion, only 123 years to reach 2 billion, 33 years more to reach 3 billion, and 14 years to reach 4 billion. On the basis of the work by the US Census Bureau, as updated in 2011, it has been estimated that the global growth rate peaked at 2.2% in 1963 and could be estimated at 1.1% in 2012 (Kivu Nature 2012). We're now at over 7 billion, and UN population projections say we even could go as high as 16 billion by the year 2100 (United Nations 2015).

Population is key, of course, as working-age population to a large degree determines, by definition, the so-called labor force. And societies need sufficient workers not only to operate, but also to generate enough income tax to pay for the services and social safety net for society as a whole: particularly for those who are not able to work by the nature of their circumstance (children, elderly population, people with disabilities, and, of course, the structurally unemployed). In much of the developed world, we are witnessing declines in population. Here is just a sampling of the industrially advanced countries that have shrinking populations: Germany, Russia, Japan, Spain, Italy, Czech Republic, and Poland. This is unprecedented in history except through famine, pandemic, war, or mass emigration. And countries with shrinking populations are, unsurprisingly, aging overall, too. So, there are fewer working-age workers to support the social safety net that protects an aging population. This situation is something new and is a major societal challenge. On the other hand, many developing countries are still growing significantly (and likely will continue to grow for a while). And they face the traditional problem of societies with growing populations (but at a scale that is unprecedented): finding new jobs on top of the already existing jobs that they hope will remain. Let's look at just one example. Just imagine the challenges that Nigeria faces. Their population, which was around 96 million in 1990, is projected to grow to around 263 million by 2030 (United Nations 2015). Think of the job market implications—even without any pressures on employment due to new technologies.

The developing world, in a globalized economy, will use the new technologies that are creating technological unemployment because the efficiencies and possibilities they create are almost required to meet the food, shelter, and other needs of these so-rapidly growing populations. But these technologies will also hollow out existing job markets just when so many more jobs are needed in addition to the old ones to provide income for all the new citizens.

The developed nations with shrinking populations can only deal with their challenges either by accepting large numbers of immigrants or having machines do the work that humans used to do. We've seen that the response to immigration, particularly cross-cultural immigration, is often not a positive one. This will increase the temptation to automate and robotize that much more. So, yet again, there seems to be something fundamentally different occurring in this era in history.

5. *In the past, average life expectancy was only around a few decades. And prime working years fit into a much shorter lifespan. In other words, the available years for a career and life that might be interrupted by unemployment are now much greater.*

Life expectancy—largely as a result of scientific and technological innovations in health and medicine—has grown over the past century to reach six, seven, or eight-plus decades, with a great extension as well to the number of active, healthy years of life. As Google engineering chief and noted futurist Ray Kurzweil said in a recent *Maclean's* magazine article, life expectancy "was 20 a thousand years ago" and "37, 200 years ago," and there is no technical reason to believe that this exponential curve will stop (Lunau 2013). New biotechnology and other medical advances are leading many scientists to think that socially transformative levels of life extension are possible in the coming decades, perhaps in only a few. At one of my WTN events, Kurzweil provoked peoples' thoughts from the stage with the following idea: we will soon be approaching the point where for every additional year that passes we will actually be adding more than a year of life expectancy. Until the full impact of medical and longevity breakthroughs spread across the world's population, that moment may be delayed. But eventually, death for most of the population, barring accidents, may become a thing of the past.

So, we live in an era when we will not only be living longer, but we will also be able to work much longer. In the past, people didn't work as many years and retired earlier, creating job openings for their younger colleagues. Technological innovation may get rid of the jobs of the several billion people currently working, who will live much longer and therefore work much longer. Technological innovation may not create enough jobs for the new billions being born if those new jobs can be performed by technology. Population, aging, and health are all, it seems, going to change the nature of society and the world of work in ways we've never seen before.

6. *The most important factor about our time that could make one believe that things are fundamentally different when it comes to the impact of creative destruction: the new technologies themselves.*

In the past, most new technologies did not have the truly transformative (and multi-purpose) power of so many of the newest technologies today or those coming soon. In the past, a human almost always did the job better. And although machine labor has always enhanced human labor or has been good at doing things that required brute strength or repetitive tasks, we have long held the place of privilege when it came to the mind, intelligence, and certainly creativity. This is no longer as true as it once was, and that is a real revolution. Perhaps, eventually, the final one.

THE PHASE CHANGE

For the past few years, I have given talks about what I call "The Phase Change" of human civilization. A phase change is when, for example, liquid water turns to ice or steam. It is when the elements are the same but also structured utterly differently. I think more change—largely driven by technological innovation—is coming to humanity in the next 20–30 years than in the past 2000–3000 years. This is a civilizational phase change. We are gaining elemental control over the building blocks of life. We are on the verge of full control over matter—with the power to make anything out of anything, anytime, anywhere. We are certainly well on our way to mastering information and data and the full range of the prose and poetry of its capacities (a form of deep magic we know so well in our own heads).

And I haven't even yet mentioned artificial intelligence (A.I.): although it may be down the road a bit as the ultimate game changer, the advent of full machine sentience is not necessary for enormous transformation of our civilization. Types of machine intelligence built along the path toward A.I. could replace an enormous amount of the need for human intelligence just as likely as it could support and enhance it. The power of these new complex technologies (advanced software, robotics, 3D printing, disintermediation via the Internet, cutting edge brain science and other medical breakthroughs, just to name a few), and the speed at which they are arriving, in almost every country, in almost every industry, with so many more people living longer and able to work longer, all this taken together means we've got an unarguably large and unique perfect storm brewing.

In short, all the assumptions of human civilization and how it has had to be structured are up for grabs. Our daily lives, our collective cultures, our politics, our economics, and certainly our work (and the nature of and need for it) have started to change in ways so profound that an entire society can seem dizzy, and the future seem unprecedentedly hazy.

To expect that all of this won't create massive unemployment challenges over the next couple of decades and beyond is either incredibly naïve or, frankly, impressively delusional. At the very least, the thoughtful observer must agree that it is indeed *possible* and perhaps *highly likely* that something is fundamentally different about our time. For all these reasons, the process of creative destruction this time around may not create more net new jobs than it destroys.

PREPARATION

So that brings us to the idea of preparation. We need to be thinking about what is happening to civilization. And we need to be exploring scenarios about what could happen. Many people, perhaps billions, will almost certainly visit dystopia in the next few decades if we ignore the implications for employment of the phase change.

The WSTU event that we at the WTN held in 2015 was arguably the first high-level, global conference and workshop for thought leaders across all disciplines and domains designed specifically to discuss the topic of technological unemployment and to begin the critical task of confronting the vast challenges ahead. The Summit's purpose was mainly to define and examine the scope of possible technological unemployment, so that there would be a later basis for proposing solutions. Nevertheless, one possible near-term solution came up repeatedly at this meeting: a universal basic income for all citizens is one idea that is drawing much attention, and which is already being tried in numerous cities in the Netherlands, all of Finland, some of Canada, and one town in Germany.

We not only captured all the presentations at this event (which are available at http://www.wtn.net/wtn-technological-unemployment-summit), but also are sending the link to the webcasts and related materials to the offices of all the world's political leaders, including presidents, prime ministers, finance ministers, labor ministers, central bank heads, and such, and we are also producing a documentary film. *The End of Employment*, by Lena Halberstadt and Eric Halberstadt, a planned film production of the WTN, built around interviews conducted with many of the speakers at the WSTU as well as at our 2015 World Technology Summit & Awards, also held at TIME Inc. headquarters less than two months later. It also contains follow-up interviews, and traces the stories of a few individuals directly impacted already by technological unemployment.

This subject of technological unemployment is too important to just let matters take their own course. Our social peace, education system, industrial forecasting, social welfare system, tax policy, geopolitical alignments, and so much more are all at play. It is not an exaggeration to say that the very character of civilization itself is at stake. As a society, we need to be asking three crucial questions:

1. What are the primary CHALLENGES we likely face regarding these issues in a world heading toward massive technological disruption of human labor?
2. What NEW STRATEGIES regarding these issues would need to be developed/created in order to address these challenges?
3. What ACTIONS should we take now regarding these issues to speed up the move to a stable and equitable society with little required human labor?

WHY WE ALL NEED TO TAKE PREPARATION PERSONALLY

It is the task of appropriate institutions, policy makers, and people like you to figure out the answers to these questions. But the truth is that the coming wave of technological unemployment is going to hit each of us individually, our families, and our society, and we are only going to do something about it—including even just thinking about it—if we care at a personal level.

Here are a few of the reasons that the issue hits home for me. Perhaps you will share some of my perspectives:

1. I am concerned for my two young daughters (age 16 and 20 at the time of this writing). Their formal education is preparing them for a world that will not exist in 5 years, let alone 10. And how do I look them in the eye and encourage their career dreams while thinking that most jobs that are done by humans today soon won't require them anymore?

2. I'm worried about some nasty politics. Almost every period of great political upheaval in the past few centuries that has involved totalitarian (on the left) or fascistic (on the right) behavior has occurred during a period, or grown out of a period, of large-scale unemployment and economic anxiety. When large numbers of unemployed people have a loss of hope and purpose, political demagogues have found it easy to manipulate them into forming a mob, or at least into unempathetic or societally negligent behavior. There are those who believe that we witnessed this phenomenon in the 2016 US presidential campaign and the resulting surprise election of Donald Trump.

3. I am hoping we make a smooth transition to the emerging new era. It is conceivable that all of these new technologies here now and coming down the pike will generate an untold level of prosperity and opportunity for humanity. My fear is that we may not make it over the unstable bridge to that future and, in doing so, will create a dystopian future or, at the very least, an unnecessarily dystopian transition. We might be able to help our capabilities expand in ways that would have shocked even the most ambitious alchemists and spiritualists from centuries past. And the scale of the changes could increase so quickly and in so many industries and other aspects of life at the same time that our cultures would not be able to adjust if we don't think through in advance about their impact. The end of the drudgery of required

work could be the bridge to an unprecedented period of human creativity. But it might not, if we aren't carefully prepared.

4. I am deeply concerned about growing income inequality. There are those who argue quite convincingly that not only is there something inherent in modern capitalism that guarantees substantial and indeed growing income inequality, but also that there is something in technological innovation itself operating within that system that does so as well. And, if we want all the innovation and all the societal wealth, productivity, and, frankly, magic that comes with it, we need to figure out how to better distribute wealth so we don't leave people behind.

And, if the percentage of people that could be out of work and left behind is potentially going to grow to unprecedented levels, then we have to figure out how to create new forms of societal support and safety nets hand in hand with our other innovations. I personally believe (as did and do many of the leading thinkers on the topic, including those who spoke at our WSTU event) that a universal basic income is required. Eliminating much of the complex social welfare system and replacing the "social safety net" (through which many have fallen) with a social safety floor with minimal, sufficient financial support to all, regardless of their current circumstances, may be the only way to avoid a social collapse. Also, it may lead to an unprecedented social flowering as the age-old condition of economic anxiety is removed. In any case, and whatever the strategy, in the face of growing income inequality, new and bold thinking is required.

5. I am concerned for myself. There is no future I've ever imagined where I did not have a purpose in my work that uses my mind, my expertise, and my passion to give my day-to-day life a feeling of meaning. I want to work. I truly want to work. I want to be relevant. I want all humans to feel relevant. And I want them (us) actually to be relevant in the coming years.

The reader may find my perspective not particularly optimistic. I like to think of myself and others as simply being conscientious in the face of a massive potential challenge to human civilization. There is a concept discussed in recent years known as the Precautionary Principle. It's basically a more formal way of thinking about the aphorism "better safe than sorry." Some argue that such a precautionary approach should be invoked particularly if the future downside of a threat is notably large, and/or impacts many people, and/or is not easily undone. A classic example of a situation where society has chosen to take the precautionary approach is global climate change. I would argue that the other potentially most disruptive threats to human civilization at the moment are the unintended consequences resulting from the transformative technological revolutions now under-way—particularly the consequence of unemployment. To not prepare for a challenge of this scale seems irresponsible to an enormous degree.

There are growing number of efforts underway to prepare for a future of technological unemployment (and this book will cover many of them in other chapters). Aside from the idea of a Universal Basic Income that I mentioned earlier, other ideas for mitigating the effects of technological unemployment include micro-taxes on some kinds of digital transactions that use open source code and reducing working hours to spread jobs among more people (Sweden is currently exploring this option). Efforts centered in Silicon Valley—such as the Vint Cerf/David Nordfors-chaired i4j (Innovation for Jobs) initiative—are explicitly seeking to use new tech-nologies to create new types of job opportunities and job markets. There is much to be optimistic about, not least of which is the previous history of humanity when it comes to creating new jobs from new technologies. Nonetheless, I am concerned for all the reasons expressed above and I invite the reader to share in that concern.

A FINAL THOUGHT

We are going to have a radically new civilization in the next few decades, largely driven by new technologies and their ripple effects. The Phase Change for our civilization is happening. Let's avoid dystopia and aim, if not for utopia, then for something much better than what we've got, some-thing much more politically and environmentally sustainable. Something for the first time ever, perhaps, that is actually morally defensible in every way. If we get creative, we can make this new civilization a better one. For everyone. Together, we can begin, finally, to redefine creative destruction.

REFERENCES

Cox, W. Michael, and Richard Alm. 2007. Creative Destruction. In *The Concise Encyclopedia of Economics*. 2nd ed. http://www.econlib.org/library/Enc/CreativeDestruction.html

Keynes, John Maynard. 2010. Economic Possibilities for our Grandchildren. In *Essays in Persuasion*, 321–334. New York: Palgrave MacMillan.

Kivu Nature. 2012. Exponential Population Growth. *The Kivu Nature Blog*, May 10. http://www.kivu.com/exponential-population-growth/

Lunau, Kate. 2013. Google's Ray Kurzweil on the Quest to Live Forever. *Macleans*, October14.http://www.macleans.ca/society/life/how-nanobots-will-help-the-immune-system-and-why-well-be-much-smarter-thanks-to-machines-2/

Marx, Karl. 1936. *Capital: A Critique of Political Economy*. New York: Modern Library.

Meade, Barbara J., Margaret K. Glenn, and Oliver Wirth. 2013. Mission Critical: Getting Vets With PTSD Back to Work. *NIOSH: Workplace Safety and Health*, March 29. Medscape & NIOSH.

Schumpeter, Joseph Alois. 1976. *Capitalism, Socialism, and Democracy*. London: Routledge.

Stewart, Ian, Debapratim De, and Alex Cole. 2015. Technology and People: The Great Job-Creating Machine. London: Deloitte. http://www2.deloitte.com/content/dam/Deloitte/uk/Documents/finance/deloitte-uk-technology-and-people.pdf

United Nations. 2015. Department of Economic and Social Affairs. Population Division. *World Population Prospects: The 2015 Revision, Key Findings and Advance Tables*. Working Paper No. ESA/P/WP.241. https://esa.un.org/unpd/wpp/publications/files/key_findings_wpp_2015.pdf

CHAPTER 4

Employment in the Age of Em: Simulated Brains and the Economics of Labor

Robin Hanson

BRAIN EMULATIONS

As supply and demand tends to be a reasonable, if rough, approximation of some overall features of labor markets, the future of employment can be seen as depending on both the future of supply and the future of demand.

The future of labor supply depends on future wealth and its distribution, on the meaning and enjoyment that workers can find in jobs, and on how attractive are the alternatives to working. The future of labor demand depends on the total size of the human population, on the distribution of labor quality, and on the quality of labor tools that can augment or substitute for human workers.

One of the most dramatic possibilities for future changes to the demand for human labor is the potential arrival of strong substitutes for human labor in the form of artificially intelligent computers. And one of the most dramatic versions of this scenario, and one of the easiest to analyze, is that of brain emulations, or "ems":

R. Hanson (✉)
George Mason University, Fairfax, VA, USA
e-mail: rhanson@gmu.edu

© The Author(s) 2017   51
K. LaGrandeur, J.J. Hughes (eds.), *Surviving the Machine Age*,
DOI 10.1007/978-3-319-51165-8_4

DEFINITION: An *em* results from taking a particular human brain, scanning it to record its particular cell features and connections, and then building a computer model that processes signals according to those same features and connections. A good enough em has close to the same overall input–output signal behavior as the original human. Once connected to artificial ears, hands, and so forth, one might talk with it, and convince it to do jobs.

Ems have been a staple of science fiction for many decades (Clarke 1956; Egan 1994; Brin 2002; Vinge 2003; Stross 2006), and have often been discussed by futurists (Martin 1971; Moravec 1988; Hanson 1994, 2008; Shulman 2010; Alstott 2013; Eth et al. 2013; Bostrom 2014).

Three key technologies are required to create ems: (1) cheap parallel computers, (2) high-resolution scans of human brains, and (3) accurate signal-processing models for all human brain cell types. None of these technologies are good enough yet, but all three seem on track to be ready within roughly a century or so (Sandberg and Bostrom 2008).

However, emulations are not the only approach by which we might achieve computers smart enough to substitute broadly for human workers. Another possible approach is to continue to write and collect better software, as we have been doing for the past 70 years.

Since the 1950s, a few people have gone out of their way to publish forecasts on the duration of time it would take software to achieve human-level abilities. While the earliest forecasts tended to have shorter durations, soon the median forecasted duration became roughly constant at about 30 years. Obviously, the first 30 years of such forecasts were quite wrong. Researchers who don't go out of their way to publish predictions, but are instead asked for forecasts in a survey, tend to give durations roughly 10 years longer than researchers who do make public predictions (Armstrong and Sotala 2012; Grace 2014).

However, it turns out that our most experienced experts who specialize in artificial intelligence (AI) research tend to be much less optimistic when asked about the topic they should know best: the past rate of progress in the AI subfield where they have the most expertise. When I meet other experienced AI experts informally, I am in the habit of asking them how much progress they have seen in their specific AI research subfield in the past 20 years. A median answer (among a dozen so far) is they have seen about 5–10 % of the progress required to achieve human-level

AI, although some say less than 1 %, and others say human abilities have already been exceeded. Such researchers also typically say that they've seen no noticeable acceleration in progress over this period (Hanson 2012).

At this rate of progress, it would take about two to four centuries for half of these subfields to reach human-level abilities. As achieving a human-level AI probably requires human-level abilities in most subfields, a broadly capable human-level AI probably needs even longer than two to four centuries, at least if we assume that we can best trust the estimates by our most experienced experts on the topic they should know best. The fact that this estimate is much longer than a century or so makes it plausible that brain emulations will be the first feasible form of artificially intelligent computers.

THE AGE OF EM

In 2016, I published a book, *The Age of Em: Work, Love, and Life when Robots Rule the Earth* (Hanson 2016), in which I attempted to analyze in great detail and scope the social consequences of cheap brain emulations. My method was to make a few simplifying assumptions, and then to repeatedly apply standard consensus results from many academic fields. I was trying not to be creative or original, other than by asking this unusual question.

In particular, I followed the usual economists' practice of assuming a low-regulation, decentralized, competitive world economy. In such a scenario, individuals and organizations act to achieve their private interests, and the net effect can be outcomes that many dislike. For example, prices can change, and technologies become adopted, even when many or most people dislike such changes. Many humans may dislike many em era changes.

I also focused there, as I do here, on positive instead of normative analysis. That is, I mainly consider what is likely to be, instead of what should be. I have little doubt that, given a detailed positive description of a future, others will step in to offer their normative opinions. But I do have reasons to worry that, if I focused first on normative arguments, others would continue on that topic without attending carefully enough to the details of this future, wherein the "devil" lies. In conversation, the normative tends to displace and overshadow the positive.

In this book chapter, I will focus on *The Age of Em*'s results for humans and their labor. But first let me summarize the overall picture painted in the book of a world of ems. The em future happens mainly in a few dense cities on Earth, sometime in the next 100 years or so. This era may only last for a year or two, after which something even stranger may follow. But to its speedy inhabitants, this era seems to last for millennia. Which is why it all happens on Earth; at em speeds, travel to other planets is way too slow.

While some ems work in robotic bodies, most work and play in virtual reality. These virtual realities are of spectacular quality, with no intense hunger, cold, heat, grime, physical illness, or pain; ems never need to clean, eat, take medicine, or have sex, although they may choose to do these anyway. Even ems in virtual reality, however, cannot exist unless someone pays for supports such as computer hardware, energy and cooling, real estate, structural support, and communication lines. Someone must work to enable these things.

Whether robotic or virtual, ems think and feel like humans; their world looks and feels to them much as our world looks and feels to us. Just as humans do, ems remember a past, are aware of a present, and anticipate a future. Ems can be happy or sad, eager or tired, fearful or hopeful, proud or shamed, creative or derivative, compassionate or cold. Ems can learn and have friends, lovers, bosses, and colleagues. Although em's psychological features may differ from the human average, almost all are near the range of human variation.

During the em era, many billions (and perhaps trillions) of ems are found mostly in a few tall, hot, densely packed (real physical) cities, where volume is about equally split between racks of computer hardware and pipes for cooling and transport. Cooling pipes pull in rivers of iced water, and city heat pushes winds of hot air into tall clouds overhead. But whereas em cities may seem harshly functional when viewed in physical reality, in virtual reality em cities look spectacular and stunningly beautiful, perhaps with gleaming sunlit spires overlooking broad green boulevards.

Ems reproduce by making exact copies who remember exactly the same past and have exactly the same skills and personality, but who then diverge due to differing experiences. Typically, whole teams are copied together, work and socialize together, and then retire together. Most ems are made for a purpose, and they remember agreeing to that purpose beforehand. So ems feel more grateful than we do to exist, and they are more accepting of their place in the world.

On the upside, most ems have office jobs, work and play in spectacular-quality virtual realities, and can live for as long as does the em civilization. On the downside, em wages are so low that most ems can barely afford to exist while working hard half or more of their waking hours. (Even ems living in virtual reality need real physical resources to pay to run the computers which implement their minds.) Wages don't vary much; blue- and white-collar jobs pay the same.

All of the copy descendants of a single original human are together called a "clan." Strong competitive pressures result in most ems being copies of the thousand humans best suited for em jobs. Most ems in these top em clans are comfortable with often splitting off a "spur" copy to do a several-hour task and then end, or perhaps retire to a far slower speed. They see the choice to end a spur not as "Should I die?" but instead as "Do I want to remember this?" At any one time, most ems are spurs. Spurs allow intrusive monitoring that still protects privacy, and very precise sharing of secrets without leaking associated secrets.

Clans are organized to help their members, are more trusted by members than other groups, and may give members life coaching drawn from the experiences of millions of similar copies. Clans may be legally liable for member actions, and regulate member behaviors to protect the clan's reputation, making ems pretty trustworthy.

Em minds can run at many different speeds, plausibly from at least a million times slower than ordinary humans to a million times faster. Over this range, the cost to run an em is proportional to its speed. So the fastest ones run at least a trillion times faster than the slowest ones, and cost at least a trillion times as much to run. Regarding the perhaps one-fifth of ems who work in physical robotic bodies, while human-speed versions have human-sized bodies, faster ems have proportionally smaller bodies. The typical em runs at nearly a thousand times human speed, and a robotic body that feels natural for this em to control stands two millimeters tall.

Faster ems have higher status, and different speeds have divergent cultures. Bosses and software engineers run faster than other workers. Because of different speeds, one-em one-vote doesn't work, but speed-weighted voting may work.

The em economy might double roughly every month or so, or even faster, a growth driven less by innovation, and more by em population growth. While this growth seems fast to humans, it looks slow to typical high-speed ems. Thus, their world seems more stable than ours. While the early em era that is the focus of this chapter might last for only an objective year or two, this may seem like several millennia to typical ems. Such ems needn't retrain much during a century-long subjective career, and can meet virtually anywhere in their city without noticeable delays.

An unequal demand for male versus female em workers could encourage em asexuality or homosexuality. Alternatively, the less demanded gender may run slower, and periodically speed up to meet with faster mates. Em sex is only for recreation, most ems have fantastic virtual bodies and impressively accomplished minds. Long-term romantic pair-bonds may be arranged by older copies of the same ems.

Compared with humans, ems fear much less the death of the particular copy that they now are. Ems instead fear "mind theft," that is, the theft of a copy of their mental state. Such a theft is both a threat to the economic order, and a plausible route to personal destitution or torture. While a few ems offer themselves as open source and free to copy, most ems work hard to prevent mind theft. Most long-distance physical travel is "beam me up" electronic travel, but done carefully to prevent mind theft.

Humans today reach peak productivity near the age of 40–50 years. Most ems are near their peak productivity at a subjective age of somewhere between 50 years and a few centuries. Ems remember working hard during their youth in experiences designed to increase and vary productivity. In contrast, peak productivity age ems remember having more leisure recently, and having experiences designed more to minimize productivity variance.

Older em minds eventually become less flexible with experience, and so must end (die) or retire to an indefinite life at a much slower speed. The subjective lifespans of both humans and slow em retirees depend mainly on the stability of the em civilization; a collapse or big revolution could kill them. Retirees and humans might seem easy targets for theft, but like today the weak may be protected by using the same institutions that the strong use to keep peace among themselves. Ems enjoy visiting nature, but prefer cheaper, less-destructive electronic visits to virtual nature.

While copy clans coordinate to show off common clan features, individual ems focus on showing off their identity, abilities, and loyalties as members of particular teams. Team members prefer to socialize within teams, to reduce team productivity variance. Instead of trying to cure depressed or lovesick ems, such ems may be reverted to versions from before any such problems appeared.

Ems may let team allies read the surface of their minds, but use software to hide feelings from outsiders. Ems must suspect that unusual experiences are simulations designed to test their loyalty or to extract secrets. Ems find it easier to prepare for and coordinate tasks, by having one em plan and train, who then splits into many copies to implement the plan. Childhood and job training are similarly cheaper in an em world, because one em can experience them and then many copies can benefit.

Ems can complete larger projects more often on time, if not on budget, by speeding up ems in lagging sections. More generally, em firms are larger and better coordinated, both because fast bosses can coordinate better, and because clans can hold big financial and reputational interests in firms at which they work.

Compared with us, ems can more easily predict their life paths, including their careers, mates, and success. They are more capable than us in most ways, including being more intelligent, energetic, charismatic, and dependable. Even if most ems work hard most of the time, and will end or retire soon, most remember much recent leisure and long histories of succeeding against the odds. To most ems, it seems good to be an em.

HUMANS

Just as foragers and subsistence farmers are today marginalized in our industrial world, during the em era humans are not the main actors driving change, but they are still around on the margins. There are plausible reasons to care more ethically about the outcomes for ems than for humans, as there are far more ems experiencing far more subjective years of life. But since most readers today seem to care more about humans in an em world, let us focus on how humans fare in the age of em.

Em cities are probably not very hospitable places for humans, and in any case real estate is far too expensive for humans to live there. However, as ems are concentrated into a small number of dense cities, humans are mostly allowed to use the rest of the world as they like. Ems only care about places close enough to em cities to be able to cheaply supply those cities with raw materials, energy, and so on.

Ems are so fast that humans will only experience days in the time that a typical em experiences years. This suggests that during the entire em era, humans will only achieve modest psychological and behavioral adaptations to the existence of ems. The human world will mostly look like it did before ems, except for a limited number of changes that can be made quickly. Ems being faster than humans also suggests that most substantial changes to human behaviors during the em era are driven by outside changes, rather than from within human society. Relevant outside changes include wars, changing prices such as wages, interest rates, and land rents, and an explosion of new products and services from the em economy.

In the em era human labor markets become very simple: they basically don't exist. That is, few ordinary humans can earn wages in competition with em workers, at least when serving em customers. A few humans might serve as celebrities because they are human, but everyone else must retire. Humans could still work for meaning and enjoyment, but not for wages. As the transition from a world like ours to a full em era may only take 5 or 10 years because of the extremely rapid rate that ems can reproduce and work, humans have only a short time to adapt to losing their ability to earn wages.

Individual humans without sufficient non-wage assets, thieving abilities, private charity, or government transfers are likely to starve, as have people throughout history who lacked useful assets, abilities, allies, or benefactors. A safe prediction is that in some places humans will do a good job of insuring and sharing, so that few humans suffer, while in other places they will insure and share much less, resulting in more humans suffering. We might hope that there will be fewer of this later set of problematic places, but we just don't know.

In our world today, financial redistribution based on individual income has the potential problem of discouraging efforts to earn income, and thereby reduce the total size of the "pie" available to redistribute. In an em economy, however, where almost all humans are retired, this problem is reduced; there are fewer incentive problems resulting from financial redistribution between retired humans.

Because ordinary humans originally owned everything from which the em economy arose, as a group they could retain great wealth in the new era. Humans could own real estate, stocks, bonds, patents, and so forth. And if the economy doubles every month, then human investments would double roughly every month. So humans would collectively get very rich very fast. (Though as we observed above, humans without assets or allies would suffer.)

Thus, a reasonable hope is that ordinary humans become the retirees of this new world. We don't today kill all the retirees in our world, and then take all their stuff, in part because such actions would threaten the stability of the legal, financial, and political institutions on which we all rely, and in part because we have many direct social ties to retirees. Yes, we all expect to retire today, while ems don't expect to become human, but em retirees are vulnerable in similar ways to humans. So ems may be reluctant to expropriate or exterminate ordinary humans if ems rely on the same or closely interconnected legal, financial, and political systems as humans, and if ems retain many direct social ties to ordinary humans.

Ordinary humans are mostly outsiders to the em economy. While they can talk with ems by email or phone, and meet with ems in virtual reality, all these interactions have to take place at ordinary human speed, which is far slower than typical em speeds. Ordinary humans can watch recordings of selected fast em events, but not participate in them.

Although the total wealth of humans remains substantial, and grows rapidly, it eventually becomes only a small fraction of the total wealth, because of ordinary human incompetence, impatience, inattention, and inefficiency. Being less able than ems, humans choose worse investments. Being impatient, they spend a larger fraction of their investment income on consumption. Fast ems are even more psychologically impatient, but they are more strongly embedded in institutions such as clans that limit independent action.

Being outsiders, humans attend less carefully to their investments in the em economy. This makes them absentee owners, who generally earn lower rates of investment return than do active and attentive owners. Today, privately held firms are consistently more responsive to changes in investment opportunities, and as a result earn on average a few percent higher returns per year than do public firms (Asker et al. 2011, 2015). While private investors suffer from lower liquidity and higher risk in private ventures, over time such investors still tend to accumulate a larger fraction of total wealth (Sorensen et al. 2014).

Some ordinary humans may own their own land and produce their own food on it, and so need to buy little from the em economy. Even so, a need to pay property taxes to em governments for "protection" could force such humans to slowly sell off their lands to pay such taxes. For example, if you paid for a 5% tax on the rental value of your property by selling off slices of that property, your property holdings would fall by half for every 20 real doublings of fully reinvested investment funds.

When humans only own a small percentage of wealth, this may help protect them from direct expropriation by ems. If ems interact with humans via the same institutions of finance, law, and politics that ems use with each other, then expropriating humans' property could threaten the reliability of the social institutions that ems use to keep the peace with each other. This may not be worth the bother to acquire such a small fraction of wealth.

This protection of human assets, however, may only last for as long as the em civilization remains stable. After all, the typical em may experience a subjective millennium in the time that ordinary humans experience one objective year, and it seems hard to offer much assurance that an em civilization will remain stable over tens of thousands of subjective em years.

But slow em retirees may at least make good allies with humans in efforts to encourage stability, as the possibility of instability in an em civilization may also be the main threat to retiree longevity.

Basic changes in which property institutions are efficient for ems might adversely affect humans. This is similar to when wealthy farmers in England enclosed what were once forager common lands—a practice that started in the sixteenth century—and similar to a possible abandonment of music copyright in our world as a response to ease of copying and sharing. Those who rely on old kinds of property can lose out when such property no longer exists.

A few objective years after an em transition, the em economy may be thousands to billions of times larger than when it started, but the population of humans *must* stay essentially the same as before, unless revolutionary new methods are found for creating new humans very quickly. Because their investments double at nearly the rate that the economy doubles, ordinary human wealth doubles roughly every objective month or faster during the age of em, greatly encouraging humans to save. This wealth can buy increasingly elaborate mansions, flying cars, and much else, though not real estate near em concentrations. Compared with serving em customers, transport of products to ordinary humans is expensive, and innovation of products targeted for humans is probably slower.

When scanning costs are low enough, wealth levels that make a human poor could make an em rich. Poor humans may have the option to switch from a life of poverty as a human to a life of leisure and comfort as a retired em. This possibility limits em sympathy toward poor humans. If there is to be any redistribution between humans and ems based on who is rich and who is poor, the transfers are likely to be from humans toward ems. Humans are mostly idle rich capitalists during the em era.

Ems may envy humans their wealth, leisure time, and more direct connections with nature, both human and otherwise. But as ems have such high abilities, they are likely to associate the styles and habits of humans with low competence. Ems may go out of their way to distinguish their styles and mannerisms from those of humans. Ems may treat humans more with sympathy, and ancestral gratitude, than with respect. They may even routinely mock humans. For example, just as brain emulations may be called "ems" for short, humans may be called "ums" for short, as this is part of the word "human" and also insultingly describes a common scenario of human befuddlement when interacting with smarter faster ems. Humans may also be mocked for their squeamishness regarding em death.

To varying degrees, humans today identify with and care about their status as the central drivers of change in the world and as being essential resources for enabling such change. An em world moves humans off of this center stage, and humans may be unhappy and discouraged by this. After all, seeing you and your friends as the center of the universe can be motivating and invigorating.

In sum, humans are no longer at the center of the world's story during the em era. But they are still around, and most can plausibly live comfortably as retirees, at least for as long as the em civilization remains stable. But, alas, it is hard to offer much assurance of stability on human lifetime timescales.

References

Alstott, Jeff. 2013. Will We Hit a Wall? Forecasting Bottlenecks to Whole Brain Emulation Development. *Journal of Artificial General Intelligence* 4(3): 153–163.

Armstrong, Stuart, and Kaj Sotala. 2012. How We're Predicting AI–or Failing to. In *Beyond AI: Artificial Dreams*, ed. J. Romportl, P. Ircing, E. Zackova, M. Polak, and R. Schuster, 52–75. Pilsen: University of West Bohemia.

Asker, John, Joan Farre-Mensa, and Alexander Ljungqvist. 2011. Comparing the Investment Behavior of Public and Private Firms. NBER Working Paper No. 17394, September.

———. 2015. Corporate Investment and Stock Market Listing: A Puzzle? *Review of Financial Studies* 28(2): 342–390.

Bostrom, Nick. 2014. *Superintelligence: Paths, Dangers, Strategies*. Oxford: Oxford University Press.

Brin, David. 2002. *Kiln People*. Denton: Orbit.

Clarke, Arthur. 1956. *The City and the Stars*. London: Frederick Muller.

Egan, Greg. 1994. *Permutation City*. London: Millennium Orion Publishing Group.

Eth, Daniel, Juan-Carlos Foust, and Brandon Whale. 2013. The Prospects of Whole Brain Emulation Within the Next Half-Century. *Journal of Artificial General Intelligence* 4(3): 130–152.

Grace, Katja. 2014. MIRI AI Predictions Dataset. *AI Impacts*, May 20. http://aiimpacts.org/miri-ai-predictions-dataset/

Hanson, Robin. 1994. If Uploads Come First. *Extropy* 6(2): 10–15.

———. 2008. Economics of the Singularity. *IEEE Spectrum* 45(6): 37–42.

———. 2012. AI Progress Estimate. Overcoming Bias blog, August 27. http://www.overcomingbias.com/2012/08/ai-progress-estimate.html

———. 2016. *The Age of Em: Work, Love and Life when Robots Rule the Earth*. Oxford: Oxford University Press.

Martin, G.M. 1971. Brief Proposal on Immortality: An Interim Solution. *Perspectives in Biology and Medicine* 14(2): 339.

Moravec, Hans. 1988. *Mind Children: The Future of Robot and Human Intelligence*. Harvard: Harvard University Press.

Sandberg, Anders, and Nick Bostrom. 2008. Whole Brain Emulation: A Roadmap. Technical Report #2008–3, Future of Humanity Institute, Oxford University. http://www.fhi.ox.ac.uk/__data/assets/pdf_file/0019/3853/brain-emulation-roadmap-report.pdf

Shulman, Carl. 2010. Whole Brain Emulation and the Evolution of Superorganisms. Machine Intelligence Research Institute working paper. http://intelligence.org/files/WBE-Superorgs.pdf

Sorensen, Morten, Neng Wang, and Jinqiang Yang. 2014. Valuing Private Equity. *Review of Financial Studies* 27(7): 1977–2021.

Stross, Charles. 2006. *Accelerando*. Washington, DC: Ace, June 27.

Vinge, Vernor. 2003. The Cookie Monster. *Analog* 123(10): 10–40.

CHAPTER 5

Building a Post-work Utopia: Technological Unemployment, Life Extension, and the Future of Human Flourishing

John Danaher

INTRODUCTION: UNEMPLOYMENT IN AN AGING WORLD

Susannah Mushatt Jones died the day I wrote this sentence. She was the oldest person in the world at the time—aged 116 years. Her life spanned three centuries: the nineteenth, twentieth, and twenty-first. As an African-American woman she witnessed profound social, economic, and legal changes in her lifetime, including the election of the first black president. She lived the last 30 years of her life in a public housing facility for senior citizens in Brooklyn, New York (BBC News 2016). She was blind and partially deaf. She was under constant care toward the end, though she maintained an active role as a member of her nursing home's tenant patrol until she was 106.

If current medical and demographic changes continue, we can expect to see more people like Susannah Mushatt Jones in the future. This has important social repercussions. Life expectancy has increased dramatically in the twentieth and the twenty-first centuries (National Institute on Aging 2011). At the same time, fertility rates have gone down across

J. Danaher (✉)
National University of Ireland, Galway, Ireland
e-mail: JOHN.DANAHER@nuigalway.ie

© The Author(s) 2017
K. LaGrandeur, J.J. Hughes (eds.), *Surviving the Machine Age*,
DOI 10.1007/978-3-319-51165-8_5

the developed world (Worldbank 2016). Countries like Japan, where life expectancy now stretches to the mid-80s and birth rates are at record lows, are facing significant social and economic problems as a result of their "super-aging" populations (Muramatsu and Akiyama 2011). If the elderly spend the last decades of their lives requiring near-constant nursing and medical care, and if there is a rapidly shrinking youth population coming up behind them, who will pay for it all? How will societies cope with this demographic shift? Call this the *super-aging society problem*.

The super-aging society problem is bad in and of itself, but it becomes even more pronounced when considered in conjunction with the possibility of widespread technological unemployment. If the predictions of authors like Ford (2015), Brynjolfsson and McAfee (2014), Frey and Osborne (2013), and others prove to be correct, then not only will shrinking youth populations in countries like Japan be required to pay for the care of the super-aging majority, they will have to do so while confronting increasingly fewer employment opportunities and greater social inequality. Now, perhaps the robots themselves can help with the care—as is already happening[1]—but is this something to be welcomed or lamented? Are there other important values at stake when we think about the intersection between aging and technological unemployment.

These are the questions that this chapter sets out to answer. In the course of doing so it presents three main arguments. First, it looks to Olshansky et al.'s (2007) case for the longevity dividend—the claim that societal benefits result from the expansion of healthy lifespan—and argues that although this argument provides a solution to the super-aging society problem when considered in isolation from technological unemployment, it becomes less compelling when considered in conjunction with it. Second, despite this there is still a good independent case for lifespan extension. Third, because of this we need to radically rethink what the ideal future for human society will look like by planning for a future in which people live longer, healthier lives but no longer work or contribute to the economic productivity of their societies.

Assumptions and Clarifications

I need to clarify some key terminology and value assumptions that motivate the arguments I am going to make. I will start with the most important—and interestingly most controversial—assumption, namely:

Value of Life Extension: All else being equal, it is better to live a longer life. This implies that, all else being equal and if possible, we should try to extend people's lifespans.

Some philosophers will shake their heads at this claim, so it is important for it to be interpreted properly. First, the "all else being equal" clause is crucial. There are certain factors that, if they hold true, could negate the assumption that continued life has value. A person could be living in interminable pain (mental or physical) that makes continued life unbearable. For this person, simply extending the lifespan might not make things better. Similarly, the obligation that allegedly follows from the value assumption—namely, that we should extend life—is not absolute. It can be overridden by other considerations or obligations. For instance, if a person does not wish to live any longer it would be wrong to impose additional life years on them against their will. We should respect their informed decision because autonomy trumps forced existence. Likewise, there are other social and moral obligations that could intervene and make it wrong to extend life. Resources are scarce, and there may be occasions when extending life comes at the expense of something even more important. Still, there are important questions to be asked as to what could be more important than lifespan extension, particularly given that continued life is usually what makes all other good things possible.

This brings us to a second interpretive point. The value assumption claims that more life is "better," but it is deliberately ambiguous as to what this betterness consists in and to whom it accrues. The obvious interpretation would be that more life is better in the sense that it results in more valuable experiences and states of being *for the person who is living that life*. But it is possible that other, more extrinsic values result from lifespan extension. These values could accrue to the person's friends and family (e.g. continued friendship), as well as to the broader society in which they live. At the same time, there could be instrumental costs to others and to the broader society that are ignored if you focus purely on the benefits to the individual. So we should be sensitive to the effects of longevity outside of the individual.

Finally, this way of characterizing the value of lifespan extension includes hedges against some noteworthy philosophical objections. For example, there are a number of philosophers who claim that the value of continued existence eventually levels off and/or reverses itself. Williams (1973) is probably the most famous purveyor of this argument. He claimed that anyone living an immortal life would reach a point in time when they became incredibly bored and no longer lived a valuable life. Others have defended similar claims about the questionable value of indefinite lifespan extension (Smuts 2011; Scheffler 2013). These claims typically center on the notion that certain essential goods (e.g. a sense of achievement or purpose) dissipate if life goes on indefinitely, or on the notion that the goods of human life require a certain degree of finitude to make sense. Nothing I say here disputes these claims. It could well be that immortality is bad and that the goods of life require finitude. I simply assume that we haven't yet extended lifespans to the point where we are at risk of undermining these goods. Thus, for the time being, and all else being equal, adding to lifespan is better than not adding to it.

This value assumption lurks in the background for the remainder of this chapter, occasionally resurfacing for defense and refinement. I will also be making use of some additional terminology that is in need of clarification. First of all I will be using the term "lifespan extension" in two distinct senses:

Lifespan Extension-1 (LE1): You extend the relatively high cost, unhealthy and "aged" portion of human life.

Lifespan Extension-2 (LE2): You extend the relatively lower cost, healthy and "youthful" portion of human life.

The first sense of the term (LE1) captures a current reality. We are already getting quite good at extending the relatively high cost, unhealthy, and "aged" (I put this in scare quotes because terms like "aged" are possibly best understood relative to some norm of lifespan; hence, as lifespan extends, what counts as aged may shift in line with the new norm) parts of life. Individuals like Susannah Mushatt Jones exemplify this mode of lifespan extension. They live extended periods of time toward the ends of their lives in states of relatively low health, heavily dependent upon the care of others. This form of life extension has been facilitated by advances in fighting diseases (infectious, heart, cancer, and so on) and in palliative care.

The second sense of the term (LE2) captures a possible reality, one that numerous futurists and transhumanist activists would like to realize (Kurzweil and Grossman 2004, 2010; de Grey and Rae 2008). This form of life extension takes issue with current approaches to medical care that don't take seriously the value of reversing or reducing the negative health effects of aging. It wishes to expand the parts of life where people are healthy and relatively less dependent on the care of others for their continued existence. LE2 is thus something that these futurists and activists think we should aim for, usually following the basic value assumption that the more healthy life the better.

It is the intersection between lifespan extension (of both varieties) and trends in employment and automation that is the central concern of this chapter. It is consequently worth clarifying some terms associated with those latter topics too. Three are particularly important

Technological Unemployment:	A state of affairs in which robots/machines/advanced AI replace most forms of human paid labor.
Polarization Effect:	The division of human forms of labor into two polarized extremes: high-paid abstract labor on the one hand and low-paid manual labor on the other (Autor 2015).
Basic Income Guarantee:	The provision of a guaranteed income to all persons within a politically circumscribed society, irrespective of their ability or willingness to work.

Technological unemployment and the basic income guarantee are relatively self-explanatory. The polarization effect might be a little more unfamiliar. It is an effect described by economist David Autor (2015). It is relevant here because some people dismiss the more extreme arguments in favor of rapidly increasing technological unemployment. Economists are often among those who dismiss these arguments because they think proponents commit the "lump of labor" fallacy, that is, they assume that there is a fixed amount of labor out there and that if machines take over existing forms of labor, humans will have nowhere left to go. This assumption is flawed because there are always new jobs coming on stream that take into account the things made possible by technology (e.g. social media consultant or machine-learning consultant). Thus, according to the skeptics, technology doesn't lead to widespread unemployment; it simply changes the employment opportunities available to human laborers. Autor's polarization effect is interesting because it effectively accepts this critique of technological unemployment. That is to say, it endorses the skeptical view that technology does not lead to widespread unemployment. It then modifies the skeptical position by pointing out that technology does have effects on the types of employment that are available and that the main discernible effect of technology on employment (at the moment) is a polarizing one: advances in IT are creating relatively few highly paid and highly educated "abstract" jobs; they are destroying middle-income, middle-skill jobs; and they are resulting in many more low-paid, poorly educated, and precarious "manual" jobs. Thus, even if we don't get to a state of widespread technological unemployment, we are entering a world of increased labor force stratification.

The existence of the polarization effect has one important implication for the remainder of the chapter. It means that many of the arguments I make will hold true if you accept polarization but reject widespread technological unemployment. This is because most of the arguments are premised upon increased polarization, precarity, and inequality, which can exist even if there are plenty of employment opportunities out there. In other words, we could have lots of jobs but because of the polarizing effects of technology, most of those jobs will be poorly paid, and will be either temporary or part-time. This will contribute to social stratification and inequality. I will occasionally highlight this when presenting those arguments.

WILL THERE BE A LONGEVITY DIVIDEND?

Return to the super-aging society problem that I outlined in the introduction. We are now able to get a clearer sense of the causes of this problem. In essence, the super-aging problem is caused by the fact that we are getting better at extending the relatively unhealthy and dependent phase of life (LE1), coupled with the fact that there are fewer young people to pay for the care of the aging population. This combination often scares policymakers and politicians. It suggests to them that it is a bad thing to further prioritize lifespan extension. It suggests that the super-aging society problem is one of the considerations that might count against or override the value presumption in favor of lifespan extension. A possible solution would be to increase fertility by some compensating measure. But this too is a concern for policy-makers because lower fertility correlates fairly consistently with higher living standards, and there are additional concerns about the resource drain created by larger global populations.

This is where proponents of healthy lifespan extension (LE2) step in. They argue that policy-makers have been focused on the wrong type of lifespan extension. If we prioritized investments into LE2 over investments into LE1 we could address the super-aging society problem without going down the route of increasing fertility. This is the so-called longevity dividend argument. Olshansky et al. (2007, 12) put it as follows:

> [A]ging interventions have the potential to do what no surgical procedure, behavior modification, or cure for any one major fatal disease can do; namely, extend youthful vigor throughout the life span. Extending the duration of physical and mental capacity would permit people to remain in the labor force longer, amass more income and savings, and thereby lessen the effect of shifting demographics on age-based entitlement programs, with a net benefit to national economies. The combined social, economic, and health bonuses accruing from a slowing of the rate of aging is what we call the *longevity dividend*—benefits that might begin with those now alive, and then continue for all generations that follow.

Following up on this, Goldman et al. (2013) model possible future scenarios in which we invest heavily in LE2 over and above LE1. They reach a number of interesting conclusions. They claim that prioritizing therapies that delay aging even by as much as 2.2 years could yield economic benefits of $7.1 trillion over a period of 50 years. By contrast, focusing on the disease prevention strategies at the heart of LE1 (e.g. prevention of heart disease and cancer) would yield diminishing improvements over the same period. They acknowledge that delayed aging could have severe economic downsides if existing old age entitlements remain in place, but claim that those downsides can be offset if we increase entitlement ages in tandem with the delayed aging effect.

We see thus, in both cases, the claim that LE2 avoids the super-aging society problem by adding additional healthy and *economically productive* years to life. When read in its common prosaic form, this argument often seems pretty persuasive and commonsensical. But when you expose its logical structure, you begin to see certain problems. For example, here's one plausible reconstruction of the reasoning underlying the longevity dividend argument:

1. It is possible to avoid the super-aging society problem by extending the healthy and economically productive years of life.
2. LE2 extends the healthy and economically productive years of life.
3. It is possible to achieve LE2 by prioritizing medical research and investment into anti-aging therapies.
4. Therefore, it is possible to avoid the super-aging society problem by prioritizing medical research and investment into anti-aging therapies.

The reasoning has a certain appeal. The second premise seems true by definition: the second form of lifespan extension is concerned with extending the relatively more youthful and healthy phases of life. The third premise is empirically uncertain, but we can grant for the sake of argument that it is true: that we really can achieve LE2 by prioritizing the right research. That leaves us with the first premise. The claim that making people stay young for longer can allow us to avoid the problem of a super-aging society seems persuasive if we presume a relatively static and unchanging economic model—that is, one in which human workers contribute the bulk of the economically productive labor, one in which this work will be well rewarded, and one in which the workers will pay their fair share of tax (or charity) toward the remaining entitlement programs.

But, of course, this presumption is exactly what is challenged by the realities of technological unemployment and the polarization of labor. If the economic model shifts dramatically over the next 50 years—to such an extent that there are few, if any, jobs for human workers (and/or the jobs that are available are precarious and poorly rewarded)—then the longevity dividend will never be paid. In other words, contrary to what its proponents believe the combination of longer, youthful lifespans will not resolve the problem of having too many older people putting a burden on society's resources, because technological unemployment and labor polarization will leave them with nothing to do. In fact, the combination of longer lifespans and increasing automation may exacerbate the problem. It would result in more people living longer and healthier lives, while being unable to make an economic contribution, and consequently reliant on the state (or charities) to sustain their existence. We don't just get an *old-age dependency* problem; we get a *whole-life dependency* problem. Policy-makers may get worried again. They may insist that LE2 cannot now be prioritized because it will drain resources over two timelines: in the initial investment phase and in the long-term (if the research succeeds in achieving LE2).

The result is that the longevity dividend argument becomes a good deal less persuasive in a world of rampant technological unemployment and labor polarization. Does this, in turn, undercut the argument for lifespan extension? It may weaken it to a degree, but this is arguably only because the longevity dividend argument rests an inappropriate amount of weight on the extrinsic, economic benefits of longevity. This is probably not where the weight should be rested. There is a simple and strong independent case for healthy lifespan extension. Many people feel its pull. The common sense view is that death is pretty bad (all else being equal), and that old age and suffering are bad too. This is supported by most leading philosophical accounts of well-being and death. Most philosophers think that death is a bad thing because it deprives you of good things you might otherwise have had (Luper 2009). Even philosophical schools of thought that argue in favor of the view that death is not bad (or not to be feared) tend to also support the view that death is "less good" than continued life (Warren 2004; Smuts 2012). Furthermore, standard experiential or objective list views of well-being tend to insist that a good life is one in which our physical and mental capacities are allowed to reach their maximum potential (e.g. Sen and Nussbaum 1993). This is something that is not possible in a state of aging, ill-health, and dependency. Combining these two views, we get a case in favor of healthy lifespan extension that rests no weight on the extrinsic economic benefits. Indeed, one could argue that this argument is truer to the real rationale and motivations behind the drive for LE2—that the longevity dividend argument is simply a convenient smokescreen, revealed to be such by the impending possibility of technological unemployment.

FLOURISHING AND WELL-BEING IN A POST-WORK AGE

Suppose this independent argument is correct, does this mean we should pursue LE2 with abandon? Supporters must contend with two objections. The first returns to the territory of the super-aging society problem. The policy-maker may concede that there are strong independent grounds (namely, the badness of death and the goodness of healthy life) for supporting investment into LE2 but still insist that we must confront the economic reality: it will result in more people being dependent on others for their existence. And since we can no longer commit to the view that LE2 will solve this problem by itself—as the proponents of the longevity dividend liked to claim—we must say something in response.

And there are several things we can say. First, this may not be a problem—at least not in the sense we understand it to be. Our assumption that we will need to pay a lot for the upkeep or support of dependent populations may itself be disrupted by the coming technological changes. As Brynjolfsson and McAfee (2014) put it, the future may be one of increasing *abundance* and increasing *spread*. That is to say, there may be greater inequality in terms of income and wealth, but the poorer populations will be living in states of machine-assisted abundance. They will have all the goods and services they could possibly require. Indeed, as I suggested earlier, this could include machine-assisted abundance in the area of care and assistance for the remaining elderly or ill populations that require it. Furthermore, there are plausible ways in which we can address the problem of increasing spread. The basic income guarantee is one such way—now recommended or encouraged by many of the leading contributors to the debate about technological unemployment. Other chapters in this book explore this policy option in greater detail (see the chapters by LaGrandeur and Hughes, and by Santens), so I will say relatively little about it here. All I will say is that pointing to the combination of technological unemployment and lifespan extension may be a boon for proponents of a basic income. Why? Because it intensifies the pragmatic concerns that motivate many of the arguments in favor of a basic income.[2] It would thus make sense for such proponents to add the economic effects of lifespan extension to their arsenal of factors that nudge us toward it.

The second objection is rather more interesting. It argues that just as the supporter of the longevity dividend saw one of their key premises undercut by the impending reality of technological unemployment, so too will the alternative supporter of LE2 see one of their key premises undercut. How does this work? I take the following to be a reasonable reconstruction of the independent argument for LE2 that I sketched at the end of the previous section:

5. It is good for people to live longer lives in states of flourishing and well-being.
6. LE2 allows people to live longer lives in states of flourishing and well-being.
7. Therefore, LE2 is good.

The problem here is that premise (6) may be less plausible in a world of rampant technological unemployment and labor polarization. This is because whatever income it may provide, paid employment is, for many people, a privileged context in which they can achieve goods that make flourishing and well-being possible. Gheaus and Herzog (2016) express the point nicely when they argue that there are four non-monetary goods that are associated with work: (i) mastery/excellence; (ii) community; (iii) social contribution, and (iv) status. The first of these is particularly important because work is often what allows us to exercise certain cognitive and physical capacities to their maximum potential, which is something intrinsic to many theories of flourishing. The problem, as Gheaus and Herzog point out, is that a basic income may not be able to compensate for the loss of these goods. Basic income lessens the monetary inequalities caused by the lack of work; it does not lessen the non-monetary inequalities such as the loss of mastery, community, social contribution, and status. So people living longer and healthier lives in a world without work may not find themselves in a world that is conducive to flourishing and well-being.

In previous work (Danaher 2016), I have argued that this pessimistic view must be counterbalanced against the fact that work is, for many people, a source of misery and frustration, and, furthermore, that there are many non-monetary contexts which allow for excellence, social contribution, community, and status to develop. Indeed, one could develop this argument and claim that a major advantage of technological unemployment may be that it allows these other contexts to assert themselves more forcefully. The reality is that paid work monopolizes our time and provides a set of incentives that frequently do not align with our interests, talents, or values (Frayne 2015). We might prefer (and be better suited to doing) more voluntary and charitable work, but be prevented from doing so by the need to earn an income. If we can break the link between income and employment, the voluntary and charitable spaces for meaningful activity might open up to us. Those spaces may then allow us to achieve mastery, work with others, contribute something of value to society, and attain positive social status, without being always beholden to the need for monetary reward. In many ways—and this is a view shared by other "anti-work" theorists (see Frayne 2015 for a review of these arguments)—technological unemployment could consequently be a major boon to our flourishing and well-being. And if we have more time (through healthy lifespan extension) to pursue these non-monetary goods, surely that is all for the better? In short, the persuasiveness of this critique of premise (6) is unsure.

Still, even I have my doubts about living a long and flourishing life in a world without work. In the remainder of the chapter I want to consider these doubts and explore a more radical possibility that could allow us to embrace the combination of technological unemployment and healthy lifespan extension, without lamenting the economic, social, or personal repercussions.

THE POST-WORK UTOPIA AS A WORLD OF GAMES

My doubts about flourishing in a post-work future rest on the possible *meaning deficit* that could arise in such a world. Meaning is a distinct component of human flourishing and well-being. It is a somewhat contested philosophical concept, but for present purposes I will focus one plausible theory of meaning, taken from the work of Thaddeus Metz (2010). This theory argues that our lives accumulate meaning when we contour our intellects to the pursuit of the good, the true, and the beautiful. In other words, when we act to bring about morally good states of affairs, pursue and attain a true conception of reality, and produce (and admire) things of great aesthetic beauty. This is a consequentialist theory of meaning. It is critical to this theory that your individual actions help to causally attain these three great states of affairs. In other words, there must be a link (typically causal and/or mental) between what you do and what happens in the world around you in order for you to derive meaning from what you do. The big problem is that the automating technologies that make widespread technological unemployment an impending reality also threaten to sever that causal–mental link between what you do and what happens in the world around you. Automating technologies, after all, obviate the need for humans in certain endeavors.

The problem then with those, like me, who insist that paid work is often boring and degrading, and that we would be better off without it, is that we tend to assume that if we can achieve technological unemployment and the basic income, then the automating technologies that make this possible will simply free us up to pursue things that provide opportunities for greater meaning and flourishing. That is the essence of the argument I outlined at the end of the previous section. But it may not work that way. There is no good reason to think that advances in automating technologies limit themselves to activities that provide less meaning for humans. In fact, we already know that technological developments affect other domains where we would like humans to remain relevant. For example, if we assume that science is the main way in which we pursue "the true" in the modern world, then there are already some obvious ways in which automating technologies are removing us from this domain of meaning. Science is increasingly a big data enterprise, in which machine-learning algorithms are leveraged to make sense of large datasets, and to make new and interesting discoveries. These systems are in their infancy now, but already we see ways in which the algorithms are attenuating the link between individual scientists and new discoveries. Why? Because these learning algorithms are becoming increasingly complex and are working in ways that are beyond the understanding and control of the individual scientists. The crucial causal–mental link is being weakened all the time.

The resulting concern is that developments in automating technologies may narrow the domain for genuinely meaningful action. There are, no doubt, meaningful activities that will remain accessible to humans (e.g. there are serious questions as to whether machines could ever really take over the pursuit of the beautiful, and one can presume that raising and nurturing families will remain an option of great meaning to many people), but the total number will diminish in the wake of rampant automation.[3] Humans could still be very well-off as a result: we could build a world of abundance in which machines solve most moral problems (e.g. curing disease, distributing goods and services, deciding on and implementing important social policies) and make new and interesting discoveries in which we can delight, and in which we are richly rewarded by their technological acceleration, but we will be the *passive recipients* of these benefits, not *active contributors* to them. There is something less-than-idyllic about such a world.

This is where we may need to radically rethink what it takes to live a long, meaningful, and flourishing life.[4] One thing that would be left open to us in this post-work future is leisure and hobbies or, what I shall here call, *game-playing*. While the machines are busy solving our moral crises and making great discoveries (assuming the advent of true artificial general intelligence), we could participate in more and more elaborate and interesting games. These games would be of no instrumental significance—they wouldn't solve moral problems or be sources of income, for example—but they might be sources of meaning and they might allow for a genuinely utopian form of flourishing.

To understand how this might happen, we need to get a better handle on what a game is. I rely on the conceptual analysis provided by Bernard Suits (2005). Suits argues that games have three key features:

Prelusory Goals: These are outcomes or changes in the world that are intelligible apart from the game itself. For example, in a game like golf the prelusory goal would be something like: putting a small, dimpled ball into a hole, marked by a flag. The prelusory goal is the state of affairs that helps us keep score and determine who wins or loses the game.

Constitutive Rules: These are the rules that determine how the prelusory goal is to be attained. According to Suits, these rules set up artificial obstacles that prevent the players from achieving the prelusory goal in the most straightforward and efficient manner. For example, the most efficient and straightforward way to get a dimpled ball in a hole would probably be to pick up the ball and drop it directly in the hole. But the constitutive rules of golf do not allow you to do this. You have to manipulate the ball through the air and along the ground using a set of clubs, in a very particular constrained environment. These artificial constraints are what make the game interesting.

Lusory Attitude: This is the psychological orientation of the game-players to the game itself. In order for a game to work, the players have to accept the constraints imposed by the constitutive rules. This is an obvious point. Golf could not survive as a game if the players refused to use their clubs to get the ball into the hole.

Games defined in this manner are not limited to sports. They include video games, board games, and other hobbies and leisure activities. For instance, getting really good at solving crosswords or Sudoku puzzles would count as game-playing under Suits's definition. So would mastering certain forms of fitness training, mental testing, or model-building. Games can be solo-affairs or can involve teams of players working together in game-playing communities. The definition is a capacious one: anything with a prelusory goal, a set of constitutive rules, and a lusory attitude will count.

Here's the critical question: can a world in which we have nothing to do but play games (so-defined) provide the basis for a flourishing life? Maybe. Suits himself seems to have thought it would be the best possible life. But Suits was notoriously esoteric in his defense of this claim.

Homo Ludens

His book on the topic, *The Grasshopper*, is an allegorical dialogue, which discusses games in the context of a future of technological perfection, but doesn't present a clear-cut argument. It is also somewhat equivocal and uncertain in its final views, which is what you would expect from a good philosophical dialogue. This makes for good reading, but not good arguing. We need to turn to the work of other philosophers like Thomas Hurka (2006) to fill in the details missing from Suits's account. By doing so, we see that Hurka argues that games are possible contributors to the good life because they are a way of realizing two important kinds of value in their purest and most idealized form.

The first value derives from the structure of means-end reasoning. Means-end reasoning is all about working out the most appropriate course of action for realizing some particular goal. A well-designed game allows for some complexity in the relationship between means and ends. Thus, when one finally attains those ends, there is a great sense of *achievement* involved (you have overcome the obstacles established by the rules of the game). This sense of achievement, according to Hurka, is an important source of value. Games are good because they provide a pure platform for realizing higher degrees of achievement. An analogy helps to make the point. Compare theoretical reasoning with practical reasoning. In theoretical reasoning, you are trying to attain true insights about the structure of the world around you. This enables you to realize a distinct value: knowledge. But this requires something more than the mere description of facts. You need to identify general laws or principles that help to explain those facts. When you succeed in identifying those general laws or principles you will have attained a deep level of insight. This has more value than mere description. For example, when Newton identified his laws of gravity, he provided overarching principles that could explain many distinct facts. This was valuable in a way that simply describing facts about objects in motion was not: there was an extra value to providing knowledge that was *explanatorily integrated*. Hurka argues that the parallel to knowledge in the practical domain is achievement. There is some good to achievement of all kinds, but there is greater good in achievement that involves some means-end complexity. The more obstacles you have to overcome, the more achievement you have. Games are special because they allow us to create ever more elaborate and complex forums for these higher forms of achievement, ones that aren't limited in their complexity like real-world means-end problems. In other words, a well-designed game can be a forum par excellence for achieving this type of value.

The second source of value in game-playing has to do with Aristotle's distinction between two types of activity: *energeia* and *kinesis*. *Energeia* are activities that are all about process. Aristotle viewed philosophy and self-examination as belonging to this sort of activity: it was a constant process of questioning and gaining insight: it never bottomed out in some goal or end state. *Kinesis*, contrariwise, are activities that are all about goals or end states. Aristotle thought that process-related activities were ultimately better than goal-related activities. The reason for this is that he thought the value of a kinesis was always trumped by or subordinate to its goal (i.e. it was always instrumental and never good in itself). This is why Aristotle advocated the life of contemplation and philosophizing. Such a life would be one in which the intellectual activity is an end in itself.

At first glance, it would seem like games don't fit neatly within this Aristotelian framework. Games are certainly goal-directed activities (the prelusory goal is essential to their structure). And so this makes them look like kinesis. But remember the goals are essentially inconsequential. They have no deeper meaning or significance. As a result, the game is really all about process. It is about finding ways to overcome the artificial obstacles established by the constitutive rules. Games are consequently excellent platforms for realizing the Aristotelian ideal. They are activities directed at some external end, but the end itself has no value; the internal process is the sole source of value. Indeed, there is a sense in which games are an even better way of achieving Aristotle's ideal than Aristotle's own suggestion. The problem with Aristotle's suggestion is that intellectual activity often does have valuable goals lurking in the background (e.g. attaining some true insight). There is always the risk that these goals trump the inherent value of the intellectual process. With games, you never have that risk. The goals are valueless from the get-go. Purely procedural goods can really flourish in the world of games.

This makes a post-work world, consisting of nothing but elaborately constructed games, look like a world that allows for a certain kind of flourishing. But is this flourishing enough? Ironically, Hurka has his doubts. While he accepts that the game-playing life allows for some flourishing, he still thinks it is of a weaker or inferior sort because the players are cut off from other sources of meaning like the good and the true. This suggests a retreat to the vision of meaning I outlined earlier. I explored this argument in previous work (Danaher 2016). There, I reached a conclusion similar to Hurka. I worried that even if we could play elaborate, socially involved games, we would lose our commitment to the consequentially

valuable ends (like doing morally good work, achieving knowledge, and producing great art) that seem so central to human meaning.

But I want to close by suggesting that Hurka and my earlier self might be wrong. There may be nothing inferior about a world in which humans are no longer concerned with things like the good and the true. Indeed, this world of elaborate but ultimately inconsequential games might be the most plausible conception of what a utopian world would look like. If you think about it, the other proposed sources of meaning (e.g. the good and the true) only really make sense in an imperfect world. It is because people suffer or lack basic goods and services that we need to engage in moral projects that improve their well-being and resolve distributional injustices. Similarly, it is only because we are epistemically impaired that we need to pursue the truth. If we lived in a world in which those impairments had been overcome, the meaning derived from those activities would no longer make sense. The external goods would be readily available to all and would no longer be a source of concern or longing. In such a world, we would expect the purely procedural goods alluded to by Hurka to be the only thing left.

And what is a world devoid of suffering, impairment, and limitation? Surely it is a utopia? And by forcing us to embrace the value of game-playing as a source of flourishing, this might be exactly what the combination of technological unemployment and lifespan extension helps us to bring about.

CONCLUSION

Where does this analysis leave us? A brief summary is in order. First, the super-aging society problem is definitely a problem: one that societies need to confront. They will not be able to confront it simply by prioritizing healthy lifespan extension over unhealthy lifespan extension, as proponents of the longevity dividend argument would have us believe. This is because that argument neglects to consider the potential impact of technological unemployment and labor polarization on its motivating premise. But this does not mean that healthy lifespan extension is unworthy of our support. It deserves our support if we grant that there is value (in most circumstances) to avoiding death and living in states of flourishing and well-being. Nevertheless, defenders of such lifespan extension still need to think about how the distributional crises exacerbated by super-aging societies and technological unemployment will be resolved. Perhaps, most importantly, they need to think about what meaning and flourishing look like in a world of rampant automation.

I have suggested that we may need to embrace a radical vision in which technological unemployment and lifespan extension make possible a utopian, game-playing mode of existence. This may seem to be a lesser, not quite as meaningful, mode of existence, but it could be the closest we can get to a utopia on earth. At the very least, the importance of achieving consequentially valuable ends is something we need to consider as we dive headlong into a future of greater automation. We need to ask whether we are happy to let machines do pretty much everything of consequence and dedicate ourselves to less consequential activity, or whether we want to wrest control back from them.

NOTES

1. In my home university, NUI Galway, there is currently a large EU pilot project taking place on the use of robots for the care of aging patients with dementia. See The MARIO Project—http://www.mario-project.eu/portal/
2. I say "pragmatic concerns" because the argument for the basic income is not a solely pragmatic one. There are several arguments in favor of the basic income that derive from philosophical accounts of political freedom. See, for example, Widerquist (2013).
3. One might respond that this argument commits something equivalent to the lump of labor fallacy by presuming that there is a finite space of possibly meaningful activities. I discuss this objection at greater length in Danaher (2016). The gist of the argument in that article is that the reasons for thinking that the lump of labor fallacy do not apply to the case in favor of technological unemployment also apply to this "lump of meaning" fallacy.
4. I was first encouraged to consider this possibility during an interview conducted by Jon Perry and Ted Kupper on the *Review the Future Podcast*. I would like to thank them both for suggesting this line of inquiry. The podcast itself can be heard at: http://reviewthefuture.com/?p=606

REFERENCES

Autor, David. 2015. Why Are There Still So Many Jobs? The History and Future of Workplace Automation. *Journal of Economic Perspectives* 29(3): 3–30.
BBC News. 2016. Susannah Mushatt Jones, Last U.S. Woman Born in 19th Century, Dies, May 13. http://www.bbc.com/news/world-us-canada-36285083

Brynjolfsson, Eric, and Andrew McAfee. 2014. *The Second Machine Age: Work, Progress, and Prosperity in a Time of Brilliant Technologies.* New York: WW Norton and Co.

Danaher, John. 2016. Will Life Be Worth Living in a World Without Work? *Science and Engineering Ethics.* doi:10.1007/s11948-016-9770-5. Accessed 3 Aug 2016.

De Grey, Aubrey, and Michael Rae. 2008. *Ending Aging.* New York: St. Martin's Press.

Ford, Martin. 2015. *The Rise of the Robots: Technology and the Threat of a Jobless Future.* New York: Basic Books.

Frayne, David. 2015. *The Refusal of Work: The Theory and Practice of Resistance to Work.* London: Zed Books.

Frey, Carl B., and Martin A. Osborne. 2013. *The Future of Employment: How Susceptible Are Jobs to Computerisation.* Oxford Martin School Working Report.

Gheaus, Anca, and Lisa M. Herzog. 2016. The Goods of Work (Other than Money). *Journal of Social Philosophy* 47(1): 70–89. doi:10.1111/josp.12140. http://philpapers.org/rec/GHETGO. Accessed 3 Aug 2016.

Goldman, Dana P., David Cutler, John W. Rowe, Pierre-Carl Michaud, Jeffrey Sullivan, Desi Peneva, and S. Jay Olshansky. 2013. Substantial Health and Economic Effects From Delayed Aging May Warrant a New Focus for Medical Research. *Health Affairs* 32(10): 1698–1705.

Hurka, Thomas. 2006. Games and the Good. *Proceedings of the Aristotelian Society* 106(1): 217–235.

Kurzweil, Ray, and Terry Grossman. 2004. *Fantastic Voyage: Live Long Enough to Live Forever.* Emmaus: Rodale Press.

———. 2010. *Transcend: Nine Steps to Living Well Forever.* Emmaus: Rodale Press.

Luper, Steven. 2009. *The Philosophy of Death.* Cambridge: Cambridge University Press.

Metz, Thaddeus. 2010. The Good, the True and the Beautiful: Toward a Unified Account of Great Meaning in Life. *Religious Studies* 47(4): 389–409.

Muramatsu, Naoko, and Hiroko Akiyama. 2011. Japan: Super-Aging Society Preparing for the Future. *The Gerontologist* 51(4): 425–432.

National Institute on Aging. 2011. *Global Health and Aging* (Report). Washington, DC: NIA/NIH/WHO. Available at https://www.nia.nih.gov/research/publication/global-health-and-aging/living-longer

Olshansky, S. Jay, Daniel Perry, Richard Miller, and Robert Butler. 2007. Pursuing the Longevity Dividend: Scientific Goals for an Aging World. *Annals of the New York Academy of Sciences* 1114(1): 11–13.

Scheffler, Samuel. 2013. *Death and the Afterlife.* Oxford: Oxford University Press.

Sen, Amartya, and Martha Nussbaum, ed. 1993. *The Quality of Life.* Oxford: Oxford University Press.

Smuts, Aaron. 2011. Immortality and Significance. *Philosophy and Literature* 35(1): 134–149.

———. 2012. Less Good but Not Bad: In Defence of Epicureanism About Death. *Pacific Philosophical Quarterly* 93: 197–227.

Suits, Bernard. 2005. *The Grasshopper: Games, Life and Utopia*. Calgary: Broadview Press.

Warren, James. 2004. *Facing Death: Epicurus and His Critics*. Oxford: Oxford University Press.

Widerquist, Karl. 2013. *Independence, Propertylessness and Basic Income: A Theory of Freedom as the Power to Say No*. New York: Palgrave-Macmillan.

Williams, Bernard. 1973. The Makropulos Case: Reflections on the Tedium of Immortality. In *Problems of the Self: Philosophical Papers 1956–1972*. Cambridge: Cambridge University Press.

Worldbank. 2016. *Fertility Rate, Total (Births Per Woman) Data*. http://data.worldbank.org/indicator/SP.DYN.TFRT.IN

CHAPTER 6

Can We Build a Resilient Employment Market for an Uncertain Future?

Thomas D. Philbeck

The most fundamental political *task of a technological world is that of
systematizing and institutionalizing the social expectation of the changes
that technology will continue to bring about.*

(Mesthene 1968)

Over the past 250 years, increasing industrialism in Europe and the United
States has transformed the types of work available to people and the meaning of labor for society. Industrialism has deeply tied people's purpose and
identities to their labor and, more specifically, their economic contribution.
Industrial capitalism, diffused through the spread of market economies, has
grown to become the driving force of modernity, appropriating technology
into its campaign for productivity. In turn, increasing productivity has, by
and large, been taken for granted as *the* way to raise the standard of living
and the overall well-being of society, and being a person of value has become
synonymous with having a productive role in the economy. At the beginning
of the twenty-first century, another transformation is emerging, born on the
back of advancing technologies and the long held commitment to growth

T.D. Philbeck (✉)
World Economic Forum, Cologny, Switzerland
e-mail: tdphilbeck@gmail.com

© The Author(s) 2017
K. LaGrandeur, J.J. Hughes (eds.), *Surviving the Machine Age*,
DOI 10.1007/978-3-319-51165-8_6

and productivity. This technological transformation, however, is challenging socioeconomic stability as it threatens our productive roles as individuals.

In short, automation technologies are inducing an increasingly foreboding feeling about the future of the labor market. By the measures of many experts, the combination of artificial intelligence and robotics could soon start supplanting human beings in the workforce, and researchers, government officials, and chief executives are earnestly anticipating unprecedented changes over the next decades (Smith and Anderson 2014). In the past five years, MIT Professors Erik Brynjolfsson and Andrew McAfee have published two very popular books on the topic of technology and its impact on the economy, *The Race Against the Machine* (2011) and *The Second Machine Age* (2014), while Carl Frey and Michael Osborne, researchers from Oxford University, have delivered two comprehensive studies on the potential for automation and the future of work (2013, 2015). According to these books and studies, the trajectory of advancing technology, combined with its role in the global economy, portends a negative impact on the demand for work—the work of humans that is.

The imperative to increase productivity for the realization of a better society remains the putative objective of the coming wave of automation. Paradoxically, however, the displacement of workers could eliminate the way in which human beings currently acquire products and services, earn a living, and exchange value. Without employment, it will be difficult to maintain an adequate number of consumers, and the value that technology could add to the economy could be dislocated from the value that society derives from the economy. If the purpose of technology becomes solely about meeting productivity imperatives, automation risks become harmful to overall social well-being. In other words, increasing productivity no longer necessarily equates to being better-off, and what has been taken on faith by many as a causal relationship could be exposed as a corollary one.

Resilience to this misalignment between economic and political ends has become a topic of our times. To be sure, these ends have never been one and the same, and keeping a balance between productivity and well-being has always been a challenge. Nevertheless, historical outcomes have encouraged the stance that technological progress and increasing economic productivity have ultimately supported the political ends of societal progress and well-being, even if progress entailed a rocky transition for society. Faced with the potential ramifications of automation, artificial intelligence, and robotics, governments are actively looking for ways to build resilience into the labor market and are unsure which policies will be the most beneficial.

Also unclear are the benefits of technology for the labor market. For example, the 2016 Oxfam report, *An Economy for the 1%*, condemns the current structure of the economy for continuing to exacerbate an unhealthy level of inequality, 80% of which, in terms of reduction of labor share of national income, is credited to the impact of technology over the past decades and which would be worsened if technology were to further drive unemployment (Keeley 2015, Bogliacino 2014). Technology's ability to reduce costs is working well for economic metrics, but not so well for social ones. This begs the questions as to whether the object of the economy is human well-being or enterprise well-being, since they may only be correlates, and whether the future of production can include sufficient room for human labor to avoid horrific levels of unemployment and poverty. Brynjolfsson and McAfee believe that the "great decoupling" of human labor from rising productivity has already taken place (Bernstein and Raman 2015), and economists, journalists, CEOs, and bloggers are pitching in, suggesting ways that we can begin to prepare ourselves for the disappearance of even more jobs.

The primary objective of this chapter is to describe and consider popularly advocated policies and tactics for building resilience into the labor market and consider whether these policies will be enough to address the issues of inequality, instability, uncertainty, and growth. Hopefully, however, this chapter will also raise important questions in the mind of the reader, such as how should people measure value in an economy where growth, productivity, and benefits are decoupled from human labor, what role would government play in providing a stable framework for society, and whether or not it is time to allow productivity and growth, coupled as they are with technologies that outstrip human abilities, to drive the economy but no longer to govern society's direction. In the following sections, we will cover potential opportunities to develop resilience through educational reform, scaling work that depends on uniquely human skills, the rise of nonstandard work, policies such as universal basic income (UBI), and even more radical approaches, such as actively cultivating a symbiotic relationship with technology. The success or failure of these measures in building resilience will be measured by whether they can generate a robust labor market, mitigate the economic shock of disappearing jobs, and whether future generations are better off than previous ones.

RESILIENCE AND OPPORTUNITY

When looking to building resilience to technological unemployment, it makes sense to identify how it is that technology creates unemployment in the first place. The most visible way, of course, is through direct substitution of an analog for human labor to fulfill a particular job description. A second way, which is already pervasive, is for digital infrastructure and software to alter processes and operations, rendering previous labor requirements outmoded. Third, technology, in the service of the economic ends of efficiency and productivity, impacts the labor market as a whole and puts competitive pressure on firms to reduce employment and employment costs. Finally, through a combination of the previous methods, technology guides the preferred models by which businesses and the overall system achieve productivity objectives. Through these forms of substitution and elimination of labor, technology has been transforming the labor market for many years. The result has been a reduction of the labor participation rate by nearly 5% since the year 2000, and an expectation of a drop of another 2% by 2024 (Ford 2015; BLS 2015).

So, how can we, in Mesthene's words, institutionalize an expectation of continuous change and prepare society for a technologically driven future? Luckily, there are plenty of suggestions for building resilience circulating in the public domain, and economists are rather optimistic that new opportunities wait on the other side of this economic transformation. From Brynjolfsson and McAfee's Race Against the Machine, to Martin Ford's Rise of the Robots, to Alec Ross' Industries of the Future and Klaus Schwab's The Fourth Industrial Revolution, the consensus seems to be that while technology may displace people or cause a "Great Restructuring," it will bring new opportunities and jobs that have yet to be conceived, and life will be better for everyone, even if it isn't measured through Gross Domestic or Gross National Product.

Alongside the sensational worry over robots usurping middle-class jobs, there are also other factors for which resilience must account. For example, the majority of the global population has not yet accessed the Internet, globalization is driving increasing competition for talent and services, and the world's population is expected to reach over nine billion by 2050 (UN 2015). All of these will add their own pressures to the labor market. Throw in the effects of climate change and geopolitical instability, and the outcome for the labor market is even harder to predict. Resilience will have to contend with the fact that meeting the targets for economic growth in the twenty-first century may not only be difficult, but they may not be the targets that are important for a society to be well-off in this new context.

Resilience to this uncertain future can take several forms: from the incremental tactics meant to help keep people employed, even if wages are not ideal, to the radical rejection of the productivity imperative and the creation of a new way of measuring well-being for societies and nations. The radical options may not be realistic, at least in the short- to medium term, and the incremental steps may not be enough in the long run as technology continues to advance and bring about change. Given the vast number of lengthy reports available on the economy and the labor market, it is impossible to touch on all the options out there or to give them the detailed and nuanced treatment they deserve. Nevertheless, here are a few of the ways suggested to help build resilience and prepare society for the changes that technology will bring.

EDUCATION

One of the important findings over the past decade has been the role that technology has played in shaping labor market demand for expertise. Researchers noticed the effects of computers and software on the labor market in the 1990s, and highlighted the effects of skill-biased technological change in the rising wages of high-skill work (Autor et al. 1998). The good news is that higher educational attainment seems to have a positive correlation with higher wages. The bad news, according to Frey and Osborne's 2015 analysis, is that technology has continued a trend of concentrating wealth in the upper ranks, leading to inequality as middle-skill-level positions in the labor market are being depleted and low-skill-level positions increase (18–21). For those in the middle, the pressure is on to either learn a lot more or learn to do something else. Without continuous education to keep pace with technological change, there is a real danger of a digital skills divide that could exacerbate the employment challenges of the future. Educational reform, therefore, is one of the most popular recommendations for creating a more resilient labor market (See David Gunkel in this volume for an expanded discussion of this topic).

A focus on STEM (Science, Technology, Engineering, and Math) education has already become a popular tactic for countries that see a labor supply shortage in these areas, and is a serious concern of the European Parliament's Committee on Employment and Social Affairs (Caprile et al. 2015). Several recent reports offer speculation as to the types of skills needed in a future where technology has transformed nearly every aspect

88   T.D. PHILBECK

of industry and society. For example, Fast Future's *Shape of Jobs to Come* highlights a variety of new job fields in areas currently being created by technology, such as bioengineering and data architecture, as well as many on the horizon, such as body part manufacturing or machine linguistics (Talwar and Hancock 2010). Access to higher education, digital literacy, and quality training in order to learn the types of skills needed for future work are ubiquitously cited measures for preparing society for the exponential growth of technology (CSIRO 2016).

For others, a focus on new topics is not enough. The UK's Institute of Directors (IoD) believes that the entire educational system needs updating to help prepare the population for a technological economy. The IoD's 2016 report, *Lifelong Learning,* advocates the increased use of technology for facilitation of and enabling access to education, the transition of UK schools away from being "exam factories," and increasing curricula that are overseen by both education and industry experts (Nevis 2016). With a global slowdown in working-age population growth and a decreasing labor force participation rate, the IoD's report sees educational curricula that focus on flexible and adaptable meta-skills as the best way forward. Whether training to augment current skill sets or going back to school to change career paths, the availability of educational programs to the public is often cited as essential. To meet this obligation, educators and entrepreneurs are looking to preparing people to fit within the coming economy and to establish relevant educational structures and curricula (Edwards 2014).

Corporate retraining is another popular tactic that can help build incremental resilience. In the World Economic Forum's *Future of Jobs* report, over two-thirds of respondent firms claimed an intention to increase training (2016, 26). Commitment to lifelong learning is an important reframing of mind as the technology requires the development of new skills to keep pace. It can be less expensive for companies to retrain employees already familiar with internal systems and committed to the mission than to recruit new employees from scratch. Company apprenticeships are another option that can substitute for educational degree programs when it comes to specialized training. This option has the added benefit of reducing youth unemployment, which is one of the most onerous unemployment subcategories. Firms are keen to reduce costs associated with employees, however, so the IoD advocates for government incentives that, in the form of tax credits, would give the push needed to encourage businesses to accelerate workplace training (Nevis 2016).

Better education is surely a safe bet for personal development and realizing a more qualitatively rich life, but the question here is whether or not education will work as a measure against technological unemployment and the inequality that technology is creating in the current economic system. After all, the evidence of skills-biased technological change has already demonstrated that technology is driving the need for higher levels of education, creating a wage gap and simultaneously increasing inequality (Bresnahan et al. 2000). Martin Ford, for example, argues that increasing the number of degrees awarded will not equate to better labor participation rates or to the increase in jobs available to qualified candidates. In his words, "the problem is that the skills ladder is not really a ladder at all: it is a pyramid, and there is only so much room at the top" (2015, loc 4065). This particular point often goes underemphasized. For example, even in Nordic countries where educational systems are considered very successful in global rankings, less than 30% of the population attains some form of tertiary education—equivalent to a bachelor's degree or higher (OECD 2015). Unfortunately, potential positions of the future such as biorefinery operatives and memory alteration surgeons (Talwar and Hancock 2010) that could make a STEM career advantageous are suited only to those with quite advanced credentials.

The majority of society that does not attain tertiary education could attempt to bolster its technological skillset, but given that high-skill jobs may also come under threat from advancing artificial intelligence, it isn't clear that this is the way forward either. Though high-quality education is now widely available for free, the MOOCs (massive open online courses) that were once hyped to be a crucial fix for providing greater educational access have unfortunately not become the key to mass education (Friedman 2014). In addition, traditional higher education now comes with a hefty price tag, and with fewer jobs and greater competition, the result may be more debt which would worsen the inequality already mentioned. In his New York Times Op-ed piece, "Sympathy for the Luddites," economist Paul Krugman underlines this broken link between technology, education, and inequality, pointing out that "education is no longer the answer to rising inequality, if it ever was" (2013). The uncertainty about the demand for future skills means that while higher levels of education may be needed for advancing technical fields, education is not likely to be enough to build adequate resilience in the face of technological unemployment.

Human Skills and Nonstandard Work

Instead of betting everything on further education in STEM, other options are focusing on what humans (still) do better than machines. Headlines such as "Robots In Your Future" (Bosworth 2015) and "When Robots Take All The Work, What Will Be Left For Us To Do?" (Wohlson 2014) may sound alarmist but, several paragraphs in, the authors readily acknowledge that humans still have unique and valuable skills and that the cognitive abilities of the newest apps and software will not be nearly as intelligent as human beings in the very near future. Thus, there will be opportunities for those who have superior judgment, empathy, and critical thinking skills to find positions where these attributes are highly valued. Other human skills, such as creativity, social awareness, and leadership, also come up repeatedly along with the potential for expanding job opportunities in healthcare and education (Ford 2015; Brynjolfsson and McAfee 2011; BLS 2015).

Healthcare and education, along with hospitality and tourism, are currently refuges for real human skills where empathy reigns and robots cannot handle the important nuances required for human interactions. Indeed, at the moment, many varieties of care workers for the elderly, infirm, and mentally unwell people appear to be the types of jobs that could expand, especially in economies that have historically neglected these members of society. Martin Ford asserts that the primary hurdles to expanding these opportunities are "educational bottlenecks" that need to be swiftly addressed (2015, loc 4450). Corroborating this, Frey and Osborne's analysis concludes that social workers, physical therapists, and rehabilitation counselors as well as health educators and medical assistants are unlikely to be automated anytime soon (2013, 57–72). In addition, both elementary education and special education, where students learn as much or more from social interaction as they do from books, could incorporate more people into the workforce should there be incentives to do so.

Personal services are also a potential space for growth in a world defined by increasing technological mediation of social and economic activity. A report from Australia's Commonwealth Scientific and Industrial Research Organisation (CSIRO) describes how the "experience economy" may hold the key to driving job creation in the future (2016, 54–55). The CSIRO report also anticipates a move to a knowledge economy that will place increasing importance on interaction skills and emotional intelligence (2016, 10). Further options for the future include jobs that take advantage of the younger generation's desire for creativity and craftwork.

A personal touch may be at a premium in the future, and a creative economy could absorb some of the labor supply, given that there will likely be a boom in developing uses for new technologies like virtual, augmented, and mixed reality games and experiences. Last, in reaction to automation and robotic production, there may be an increasing number of people who desire unique goods that are not manufactured by machines, providing a renewed interest in craftsmanship.

In the short run, the absorption rate may be able to be bolstered by increasing incentives in these human-centered areas of the economy. Nevertheless, scaling these areas also has its limits. A labor market saturated with elementary school teachers, nurses, physical therapists, and personal trainers would naturally increase the competition and likely lower the wages in these fields. As the population ages, it makes sense that demand for personal care and attendants will increase, but what type of compensation can be expected? According to US News Jobs Rankings, personal care aides earn a median salary of around $20,000, some $30,000 less than the US median (US News 2016). Scaling this type of job field would threaten to diminish the returns to a point that might not make it a viable career choice at all. If the economy continues to lose mid-level positions, as the current data indicate, then those with mid-level skills and mid-level salaries will have to compete with lower-skill positions and opt for lower wages, reinforcing the inequality that resilient measures are meant to buffer against.

Despite the widespread speculation about what types of jobs might come to pass, there is not yet an equivalent to the automobile or textile industries that employed millions during the expansive decades of the twentieth century. In addition, the increases in efficiencies that have accompanied technology in the economy have helped change the priorities of firms, with regard not only to the needed skill sets, but also to their needs to drive down costs and remain competitive. Companies have had to systematically look at the cost of technologies versus the cost of employing people, the latter of which includes a variety of taxes, required insurances, and benefits. Despite the resulting pressures on workers, resilience has been developed as a matter of necessity, and the proportion of nonstandard work arrangements by companies have increased from an average of around 14% at the turn of the millennium to more than 20% by 2011 (Cappelli 2013, 578). Nonstandard employment represents an area that is hard to gauge and could possibly represent a place to absorb displaced workers.

Undeniably, workers have shown their ingenuity in utilizing technology to find new opportunities and freelance contracts to make up for the lack of available full-time employment. Unfortunately, the varieties of alternative work arrangements are not yet as able to supply the kinds of securities previously enjoyed by full-time employment. In the UK, for example, around 14% of employment is classified as "insecure work" and includes variable shifts, temporary, zero-hour contracts, and other ambiguous relationships with employers (Allen 2016). Furthermore, in the United States, more than 30% of workers are now engaged in some form of freelance or temporary employment, and the estimate is higher for other regions of the world (ILO 2013). The normalization of temporary work, lack of benefits, and independent contracting has been pejoratively labeled the "gig" economy and is expected to grow to over 40% of all jobs by 2020 (Ambrosino 2016). Though these arrangements have some advantages, they are primarily the result of satisfying businesses' incentives to lower costs, gain greater flexibility, and employ new technologies or some combination of the three (ILO 2015b, 3).

Flexible nonstandard work arrangements can be beneficial, but most often come at a cost to the well-being of employees. On average, nonstandard workers earn less for the same work as a full-time employee, are not compensated to make up for lack of social security coverage, and are less likely to receive the benefits of training programs sponsored by employers (ILO 2015b, 26–27). These adaptations in the labor market are clearly aligned with the increasing impact of technology on the economy, and represent a short-term adjustment pointing to a bigger issue, namely, that a technologically mediated economy doesn't have the well-being of human beings as its goal. Insofar as people can be expunged to advance productivity through the lowering of costs, the ends of the system as it stands now will seek to do so. From this perspective, nonstandard work, while representing the ingenuity and adaptability of the workforce, is still not a viable option for developing a bona fide resilience to technologically driven unemployment.

Policies and Regulation

Labor market policy can make an important difference in how nations are able to respond to technology driven unemployment. Since the 2008 financial crisis, fostering job creation to mitigate rising unemployment has been a highly visible policy stance in Europe (See Stevens and Marchant in this volume for further discussion of policy and regulation). The United States has been a leader in the attempt to spur new businesses and job creation by fostering entrepreneurship, and Europe has also turned to entrepreneurship as one way to meet growth expectations and counteract unemployment that has grown 65% since 2007 (OECD 2016). The *Entrepreneurship 2020 Action Plan* (2013) sets out guidelines to reduce administrative burdens, support educational institutions, and provide better access to finance for entrepreneurs. The underlying idea is to create an atmosphere that is more competitive and friendly to start-ups, resembling that of the United States. Sustaining environments where entrepreneurs can materialize their creative ideas may not fully supply the number of jobs needed to buffer technological unemployment, but it is one way to help preserve flexibility in a labor market and keep ideas open to new possibilities as technology plays a more widespread role.

Brynjolfsson and McAfee propose several policies that are indirectly related to mitigating technological unemployment, such as raising teacher salaries, creating better platforms for connecting employers to potential employees, and investing in infrastructure (2014). Raising salaries could bring new expertise and ideas into an educational structure that is highly outdated. Creating platforms for matching talent supply to talent demand could also be part of the solution against potential unemployment, by increasing the speed at which people can find and transfer to new work. Digital platforms are a recurring and successful approach to matching markets of all kinds, and there is no reason that technology cannot be a part of the employment solution. In addition, investment in infrastructure is a common policy recommendation, as it could absorb displaced workers, at least in the short term. It has the benefit of employing many people immediately, and also of preparing a country to make the most of future opportunities. With interest rates as low as they are, Ford argues there's no time like the present (2015, loc 4450).

Another favored policy is to tax the technology companies and those that rely heavily on technological substitutions for labor. This type of policy is aimed at the biased tax frameworks that penalize those who employ human beings the most. If businesses that utilize technology, especially automated technologies and artificial intelligence, need not pay employment taxes, social security benefits, or unemployment insurance, then the incentives are clearly weighted toward investing in automation, reducing the workforce, and lowering labor costs. Furthermore, funding social welfare programs on the back of payroll taxes can give technology-dependent companies a free ride (Ford 2015, loc. 4471). Thus, it would make sense to even out the distribution of the tax burden across companies of all kinds based on other criteria, perhaps such as yearly earnings or profit margins.

Theoretically, policy implementation could also take on seemingly Luddite measures, such as restricting particular technologies from being utilized in markets that employ large numbers of people. This might seem like a reactionary response, but massive layoffs from the departures of entire industries have left long-lasting marks on some communities. Derek Thompson describes the effects of the steel industry leaving Youngstown, Ohio, in a recent *Atlantic* article "A World Without Work," and he stresses how cultural cohesion can be one of the many casualties when jobs disappear *en masse*. The trucking industry could soon face this scenario, and there would be a great loss of livelihoods and tax revenues as 1% of the workforce and their support economies disappear (Peterson 2016). Generally considered, however, this type of approach is the least favored, primarily because reactionary policies don't have a very good track record, but also because there are as many optimistic visions for a future with technology as there are pessimistic ones, and fostering an open society based on market principles means letting this work itself out without grandiose measures of interference.

In addition to targeted taxation and mechanisms to help spur job creation and transition, building a robust unemployment system and a social safety net to support retraining and labor mobility may be beneficial. This is especially true in Europe, where nonstandard employment required the highest number of labor market policy regulations between 2008 and 2013, accounting for 22% of the total share of policy measures (ILO 2015a). Nicolas Colin and Bruno Palier advocate a "flexicurity" approach that would mitigate the risk of technological unemployment by decoupling employment benefits from work. The underlying principle for this approach is that those who have few benefits from employment and those that have many are both incentivized to remain tied to their work, because both groups stand to lose a great deal if they break from employers. Those with few benefits need all the money they can get and cannot transition easily, due to loss of wages having severe and immediate impact on their lives. Those with many benefits are usually deeply invested in, and tied to, their jobs in this way, and "switching costs" are prohibitive. Thus, both have incentives to stay rather than change. Colin and Palier speculate that separating benefits and social security from work would free people to take risks, create businesses, and change jobs, all of which would enhance resilience to economic shocks. Lastly, opening borders for the free flow of talent and data is also a widely mentioned policy, and providing free access to a variety of data has been taken up by France as a way to identify new opportunities, spur innovation, and increase economic efficiency (Lemaire 2016).

Unfortunately, without a systematic approach to building a social safety net, high numbers of people doing freelance and nonstandard work put the economy in a precarious situation when hit by a shock like the 2008 financial crisis. For those with low mobility due to debt or who cannot compete due to lack of expertise, insufficient unemployment benefits and social welfare assistance measures mean prolonged adjustment timelines. For jobs that are likely to have reduced wages due to labor market saturation, subsidies to wages may even be needed to reinforce resilience. If people aren't earning enough, they will either have to stop consuming or rely on debt, either of which would have negative impacts on the flexibility and adaptability of the labor market.

Basic Income

Most economists are optimistic that unemployed humans will find other occupations in which to resituate, but there is also a deep understanding that rising inequality is linked to the role of technology in the economy. As technology centralizes systems, drives wealth into the hands of the few, and begins to supplant human workers, there will be a need to manage the disparity between the "winners and losers," as Brynjolfsson and McAfee put it in *The Second Machine Age*. After all, the productivity gains of many technological businesses, especially Internet-related ones, are connected to the data and action of users who are not paid for their services (See LaGrandeur and Hughes' and Santens' chapters in this volume for more details on this topic). One clear sign of the recognition that these gains need redistribution is the reemergence of the discussion over UBI, also frequently called basic income guarantee (BIG).

Policies and metrics that decouple social opportunity and mobility from the effects of technology, such as lower wages and reduced job opportunities, would be the ultimate form of resilience. They are also the least likely to occur. UBI, however, has been under discussion, and it even made it to the level of national referendum in Switzerland, though it lost resoundingly (van Parijs 2016). One advantage of UBI would be its ability to provide some redistribution of the wealth generated by technologically driven companies. Also, Martin Ford argues that UBI providing everyone in the UK with a base of £10 k per year would help pull people out of the poverty trap caused by rising technological unemployment, increase consumption and would also be able to pay for itself (loc. 4376). While the proposal is not a new idea, it has been gaining visibility in the press, and has even been supported by one of the most well-known and respected business founders in Germany, Götz Werner, whose empire of drug stores, DM, employs more than 50,000 people (Mescoli 2016). The popularity of UBI, driven by the idea it could somehow replace the losses of social security and benefits that come with nonstandard work and rising inequality, demonstrates the crucial nature of these aspects of employment for social well-being.

With more and more workers partaking in the gig economy with no safety net, proponents of UBI argue that a life of economic uncertainty is driving fear and insecurity, leading to many problems for society (Flowers 2016). Furthermore, with technology set to displace human workers, covering basic living expenses for those out of work would help to provide enough breathing space for people to transfer to another equitable position (for more detail on UBI see also LaGrandeur and Hughes, and Santens in this volume). If UBI could guarantee this type of social support, it would indeed be one option for building resilience into the labor market. Unfortunately, there are many reasons it might not work, even if implemented. In a 2015 MIT Technology Review article "Who will own the Robots," David Rotman points out that finding a way to provide people with the money that they will then have to spend on retraining in order to adapt to the disappearance of jobs puts an undue financial burden on society, not to mention that giving the money out doesn't do anything to replace the jobs that have disappeared in the first place. Indeed, the potential benefits of UBI are attractive, but far from guaranteed.

One area of concern is that UBI may require accompanying regulation to keep rent seekers from absorbing the extra inflow of money into society. Martin Ford supplies the example of tuition costs that rose over 900% in just 15 years compared to the 135% rise in the UK's consumer price index (loc. 2427). This dramatic rise has accompanied the ready availability of student loans, and the situation is very similar in the United States. Rent-seeking behavior could quickly nullify the additional income for many people, especially in areas where demand is high and markets are trapped. A great deal of forethought would be required for the types of accompanying regulations needed to curb inflating prices, and the argument could be made that neither increasing prices nor increasing opportunities for taking on debt are likely to add to building resilience into the workforce.

Perhaps more important than all the quantitative arguments that could be made is the necessity to come to terms with the ideals of labor and competition that are engrained in the liberal market societies of Europe and North America, that is, the basic idea that human beings are, at their core, workers and that work is what fulfills and realizes the potential of people and society. In the West, this idea is tied to the economy and production, and is clearly visible in articles such as David Freedman's "Basic Income: A Sellout of the American Dream" (2016). Work has been the way out of poverty and the way to a better life in the United States, and UBI can be seen as a policy that encourages people to give up on the dream and on work as the way to a better future. Admittedly, what occupations would look like, as opposed to jobs, or how it might change things for the better if people were liberated from the burden of labor, is as scary as it is intriguing. Ultimately, GDP still rules the game from this perspective in the sense that this view is intimately tied to the economic ends of productivity, to the good of the economic machine, rather than the good of the laborer. But this may be changing.

In 2009, the European Commission established a roadmap for an initiative called Beyond GDP, and it has developed social progress indicators to complement GDP as a measure of well-being. The initiative works to develop new definitions of welfare and to challenge growth as the solely relevant model for the economy (European Commission 2016). In fact, the World Economic Forum series of the same name, *Beyond GDP*, has put the productivity imperative under the lens, and economists such as Stewart Wallis and Richard Easterlin have offered up alternative measures for considering the well-being of society that are decoupled from productivity and wage rates (Wallis 2016; Easterlin 2016). This year in Davos, the head of the IMF, Christine Lagarde, economist Joseph Stiglitz, and Erik Brynjolfsson critiqued GDP as a measure of well-being, with Brynjolfsson expressing that "it is quite possible for GDP to go in the opposite direction of welfare" (Thomson 2016). This critical assessment of GDP is fundamental, as many of the proposed measures for building resilience provide incremental steps to help keep the labor market capable of productive work within the bounds of current metrics. UBI could be a first step, and a radical one, toward decoupling wages and benefits from labor and to rethinking what the value of human beings in society looks like, but it is clear that it cannot do so as an isolated policy.

A CYBORG STRATEGY

Most measures for building resilience, such as labor market policies and scaling human-centered jobs, defend against the effects of increasing technological change by keeping a distance between technology and human beings. Education is discussed as a measure of defense against obsolescence and a way to maintain a controlling relationship with technology. The focus on human-centered jobs implicitly frames robotics and AI as substitutes and invaders rather than complements. In contrast to this, however, another perspective has emerged, suggesting the best strategy for building a resilient labor market is to intensify the commitment to technology through deeper investment and perhaps an even more intimate fusion of technology and people. For example, a McKinsey Global Institute report recommends greater adoption of technologies and fostering of technical expertise as a way to unlock steep rises in national and global productivity, as well as increase employment (Labaye and Remes 2015). Suggestions include preparing to take advantage of the Internet of Things (IoT) and cultivating sweeping transparency of data and global flows of people and services to spur innovation.

Alec Ross, in *The Industries of the Future,* surmises that the major employment opportunities of the future will accompany big data and domain expertise. He cites examples of China's investment in robotics and genomics as ways of developing industry hubs equivalent to California's Silicon Valley (2016). The way to exploit and drive these opportunities is to invest, build research and commercial networks, and commit to these technologies as drivers of the future. Becoming the administrators and creative architects of this space may hold more opportunity than we now know. A notable Silicon Valley CEO, Elon Musk, has suggested the need to fuse biology with technology, adding a layer of artificial intelligence to our brain power, so as not to become obsolete beings (Bergen 2016). Respected technology gurus, such as Kevin Kelly, the founder of Wired Magazine, are convinced that biotechnological integration is the future. Kelly remarks that we "need to civilize and tame new inventions in their particulars. But we can do that only with deep engagement, firsthand experience, and a vigilant acceptance" (2016, 5).

Truly creating a cyborg merger between technology and humans in order to continue meet productivity goals is a radical suggestion, and it may be frightening to some. The fact of the matter is that current global economic situation is ripe for a radical response to the competition people will face if the economic system does not manage the decoupling of economic ends from human labor. While most analyses are looking at incremental tactics as a way of dealing with the compound and interrelated issues, Musk and Kelly offer the "if you can't beat 'em, join 'em" strategy. So long as the productivity imperative still holds sway and the attempt to meet the growth model is still exerting massive pressure, even as all signals point to nearly impossible targets, deeper commitment offers the hope of having technology play a saving role (Labaye and Remes 2015, 51). It isn't hard to picture a future where wearables, implantables, and smart drugs are part of our daily "systems maintenance," helping us keep our bodies and minds in optimal condition for economic fitness. In such a future, the productivity imperative will have fully appropriated people, as technology transgresses the limits of human bodies for the purpose making humans better workers.

Dystopian science fiction consequences aside, supporting science and investing in technological infrastructure can be as much of a solution to future ills as it is a potential threat to current jobs. Society is more aware than ever of the binding relationship between technology and human beings and that this relationship is unlikely to become less interdependent. As biotechnology advances, there may be pressure to use it to compete for social standing and for economic rewards, and most are aware that the benefits will accrue more quickly to those who can afford the technological enhancements. Again, humanity would be faced with a situation where biotechnology employed for economic ends reinforces social discrimination and stratification.

Already, experts recognize that exploring a more interconnected future will require great forethought and serious attention to governance (Wallach and Marchant 2015). Though the potential for dystopian consequences is present, so is the opportunity for some of the utopian outcomes long wished for in regard to casting aside the burden of work. Overall, technology has sustained the transition from a manufacturing to a knowledge economy, at least in some nations, but it is unclear if technology will be able to sustain a global-scale transformation that extensively reduces the need for traditional labor. If biotechnology becomes the only hope of attaining the high-level skills for high-paying jobs of the future, the division caused by skills-biased technological change will only increase, and then both technology and society will have been thoroughly appropriated by a merely economic orientation.

CONCLUSION

Former US Treasury Secretary Lawrence Summers has said that greatest economic challenge of the future will not be production, but rather providing jobs (Summers 2014). This was echoed by the United Nations Chair of the General Assembly body dealing with economic and financial matters, Abdou Salam Diallo, in his reference to the International Labor Organization (ILO) calculation that 470 million jobs will need to be created between 2015 and 2030 just to keep up with the rising working-age population (UN 2013). Contemplating these challenges in the light of the Bureau of Labor Statistics (BLS) data that show the 2000s as a "lost decade" in the United States that produced no new jobs and ended a six-decade growth trend does not instill a great deal of confidence that we are on the right path (Washington Post 2010). Furthermore, the arguments that rely on faith that people will find something to do or that jobs will materialize in the future because they always have in the past are not overly convincing either. Society has seen the outcome of logic that says what held in the past will hold in the future in the housing crash and financial crisis less than a decade ago.

The threat to jobs and opportunities is real, though the long-term outcomes from this threat are not yet clear. Building resilience to the coming wave of automation and technological transformation entails recognizing the systemic effects of the economy's productivity imperative and how it continues to shape society through technology. Economists, such as Joseph Stiglitz, Robert Reich, and Thomas Piketty, as well as writers, such as Douglas Rushkoff, have been consistently critical of the negative impacts of traditional economic incentives. But momentum has championed technology-backed growth above all else. Society is feeling the consequences and asking where the priorities of our political system lie. The variety of options presented in this chapter is not exhaustive, and none of the options would be successful in isolation. Moreover, none of them seriously considers that the growth model may not be a desirable end in a technologically mediated society. They do, however, illuminate the difficulty and scope of the technological transformation of the economy and society, and the challenge of reconceptualizing how we value ourselves in relation to work.

Will these suggestions generate a robust labor market, mitigate the economic shock of disappearing jobs, and help make future generations better off? I'm not completely convinced. The only radical suggestion posed, that of making an even deeper commitment to technology in both existential and economic ways, still endorses a paradigm that connects the value of people to productivity. GDP, however, is no longer a reliable litmus test for well-being, and the growth model that has dominated for so long has the potential to lead to a tragedy of the commons, wherein interested parties destroy the basis for societal well-being. The EU's *Beyond GDP* indicators and the "flexicurity" that characterizes the Nordic countries could be a good first step in building a deep and longer lasting resilience, but the willingness to critically address long-held assumptions will be necessary in many nations. There is an opportunity here to remake the economy into something less self-interested and more values-driven. Perhaps new forms of employment, new metrics, and a conscious decoupling of our collective sense of identity from the work that we do could lead us toward a new consciousness in which we allow technology to produce goods and reframe our own sense of meaning toward helping one another. The new economic focus could be bringing benefits to one's neighbor as much as to oneself, a focus on distribution over production, perhaps. Such a strategy would build resilience in the labor market through diversification of resources and knowledge, and by coupling rewards to equality and fairness.

REFERENCES

Allen, Katie. 2016. Nearly One in Six Workers in England and Wales in Insecure Work. *The Guardian*, June 13. Money sec. https://www.theguardian.com/money/2016/jun/13/england-wales-zero-hours-contracts-citizens-advice-insecure-work

Ambrosino, Brandon. 2016. The Gig Economy Is Coming. You Probably Won't Like It. *The Boston Globe*, April 20. https://www.bostonglobe.com/magazine/2016/04/20/the-gig-economy-coming-you-probably-won-like/i2F6Yicao9OQVL4dbX6QGI/story.html

Autor, David. 2010. *The Polarization of Job Opportunities in the U.S. Labor Market: Implications for Employment and Earnings*. Center for American Progress and the Hamilton Project. MIT Department of Economics and National Bureau of Economic Research, April. http://economics.mit.edu/files/5554

Autor, David H., Lawrence F. Katz, and Alan B. Krueger. 1998. Computing Inequality: Have Computers Changed the Labor Market? *The Quarterly Journal of Economics* 113(4): 1169–1212.

Bergen, Mark. 2016. Here's the Cyborg Tech That Elon Musk Says He'll Do If No One Else Does. *Recode*, June 2. http://www.recode.net/2016/6/2/11837544/elon-musk-neural-lace

Bernstein, Amy and Anand Raman. 2015. The Great Decoupling: An Interview with Erik Brynjolfsson and Andrew McAfee. *Harvard Business Review*, June. https://hbr.org/2015/06/the-great-decoupling

Bogliacino, Francesco. 2014. Inequality and Europe 2020. *Intereconomics* 49(5): 288–294.

Bosworth, James. 2015. Robots in Your Future. *Americas Quarterly*. http://www.americasquarterly.org/content/robots-your-future

Bresnahan, Timothy F., Erik Brynjolfsson, and Lorin M. Hitt. 2000. Information Technology, Workplace Organization, and the Demand for Skilled Labor: Firm Level Evidence. Draft Paper for publication. http://ebusiness.mit.edu/erik/itw-final.pdf

Brynjolfsson, Erik, and Andrew McAfee. 2011. *Race Against The Machine: How the Digital Revolution is Accelerating Innovation, Driving Productivity, and Irreversibly Transforming Employment and the Economy.* Lexington, MA: Digital Frontier Press.

———. 2014. *The Second Machine Age: Work, Progress, and Prosperity in a Time of Brilliant Technologies.* New York: W. W. Norton & Company.

Capelli, Peter, and J.R. Keller. 2013. Classifying Work in The New Economy. *Academy of Management Review* 38 (4): 575.

Caprile, Maria, Rachel Palmén, Pablo Sanz, and Giancarlo Dente. 2015. *Encouraging STEM Studies: Labour Market Situation and Comparison of Practices Targeted at Young People in Different Member States.* European Parliament. Directorate General for Internal Policies Policy Department A: Economic and Scientific Policy. IP/A/EMPL/2014–13 PE 542.199 EN. Brussels. http://www.europarl.europa.eu/RegData/etudes/STUD/2015/542199/IPOL_STU(2015)542199_EN.pdf

Carr, Nicholas. 2014. Should the Laborer Fear Machines? *The Atlantic,* September 29. http://www.theatlantic.com/business/archive/2014/09/should-the-laborer-fear-machines/380476/?single_page=true

Colin, Nicholas and Bruno Palier. 2016. The Next Safety Net: Social Policy for a Digital Age. *Foreign Affairs,* July/August. https://www.foreignaffairs.com/articles/2015-06-16/next-safety-net

Commonwealth Scientific and Industrial Research Organisation (CSIRO). 2016. *Tomorrow's Digitally Enabled Workforce: Megatrends and Scenarios for Jobs and Employment in Australia Over the Coming Twenty Years.*

Decreuse, Bruno. 2001. Can Skills Biased Technological Change Compress Unemployment Rate Differentials Across Education Groups? *Journal of Population Economics* 14: 651–667.

Easterlin, Richard. 2016. The Science of Happiness Can Trump GDP As a Guide for Policy. *World Economic Forum Agenda.* https://www.weforum.org/agenda/2016/04/the-science-of-happiness-can-trump-gdp-as-a-guidefor-Policy

Edwards, David. 2014. American Schools Are Training Kids for a World That Doesn't Exist. *Wired,* October 17. http://www.wired.com/2014/10/on-learning-by-doing/

European Commission. 2016. *Beyond GDP.* http://ec.europa.eu/environment/beyond_gdp/index_en.html

————. Communication from the Commission to the European Parliament, the Council, the European Economic and Social Committee and the Committee of the Regions. 2013. *Entrepreneurship 2020 Action Plan Reigniting the Entrepreneurial Spirit in Europe.* COM(2012) 795 final, Brussels. http://eur-lex.europa.eu/legal-content/EN/TXT/PDF/?uri=CELEX:52012DC0795&from=EN

European Parliament. 2009 *GDP and Beyond: Measuring Progress in a Changing World.* COM(2009) 433 final, Brussels. http://eur-lex.europa.eu/legal-content/EN/TXT/PDF/?uri=CELEX:52009DC0433&from=EN

Feenberg, Andrew, and Michael Callon. 2010. *Between Reason and Experience: Essays in Technology and Modernity.* Cambridge, MA: MIT Press. Kindle Edition.

Flowers, Andrew. 2016 What Would Happen If We Just Gave People Money? *FiveThirtyEight,* April 25. https://fivethirtyeight.com/features/universal-basic-income/

Ford, Martin. 2015. *The Rise of the Robots: Technology and the Threat of Mass Unemployment.* London: Oneworld Publications. Kindle Edition.

Freedman, David H. 2016. Basic Income: A Sellout of the American Dream. *MIT Technology Review,* June 13. https://www.technologyreview.com/s/601499/basic-income-a-sellout-of-the-american-dream/

Freelancers Union and Upwork. An Independent Study. 2015. *Freelancing in America.* https://www.upwork.com/i/freelancinginamerica2015/

Frey, Carl Benedikt, and Michael Osborne. 2013. The Future of Employment: How Susceptible Are Jobs to Computerisation? Oxford Martin School Working Paper. http://www.oxfordmartin.ox.ac.uk/downloads/academic/The_Future_of_Employment.pdf

————. 2015. *Technology at Work: The Future of Innovation and Employment.* Citi GPS: Global Perspectives and Solutions. Oxford Martin School, February. http://www.oxfordmartin.ox.ac.uk/downloads/reports/Citi_GPS_Technology_Work.pdf

Friedman, Dan. 2014. The MOOC Revolution That Wasn't. *Techcrunch,* September 11. https://techcrunch.com/2014/09/11/the-mooc-revolution-that-wasnt/

Goos, Maarten, and Alan Manning. 2007. Lousy and Lovely Jobs: The Rising Polarisation of Work in Britain. *The Review of Economics and Statistics* 89(1): 118–133.

Goos, Maarten, Alan Manning, and Anna Salomons. 2009. Job Polarization in Europe. *American Economic Review: Papers & Proceedings* 99(2): 58–63 .http://www.aeaweb.org/articles.php?doi=10.1257/aer.99.2.58

Gownder, J.P. 2015. *2025: Working Side by Side with Robots: Automation Won't Destroy All the Jobs, But It Will Transform the Workforce—Including Yours.* Forrester Research, August 24. https://www.forrester.com/report/The+Future+Of+Jobs+2025+Working+Side+By+Side+With+Robots/-/E-RES119861

International Labour Organization. 2013. *Global Wage Report 2012/13: Wages and Equitable Growth*, Geneva. http://www.ilo.ch/global/research/global-reports/global-wage-report/2012/WCMS_194843/lang--en/index.htm
———. 2015a. *Inventory of Labour Market Policy Measures in the EU 2008–13: The Crisis and Beyond*, Geneva. http://www.ilo.org/wcmsp5/groups/public/---dgreports/---inst/documents/publication/wcms_436119.pdf
———. 2015b. *Report for Discussion at the Meeting of Experts on Non-Standard Forms of Employment*, Geneva, February, 16–19. Non-standard forms of employment, Conditions of Work and Equality Department, Geneva. http://www.ilo.org/wcmsp5/groups/public/---ed_protect/---protrav/---travail/documents/meetingdocument/wcms_336934.pdf
Keeley, Brian. 2015. *Income Inequality: The Gap Between Rich and Poor*, OECD insights. Paris: OECD Publishing. doi:10.1787/9789264246010-en.
Kelly, Kevin. 2016. *The Inevitable: Understanding the 12 Technological Forces that Will Shape Our Future*. New York: Penguin Random House. Kindle Edition.
Krugman, Paul. 2013. Sympathy for the Luddites. *New York Times*, June 13. http://www.nytimes.com/2013/06/14/opinion/krugman-sympathy-for-the-luddites.html?_r=2
Labaye, Eric, and Jaana Remes. 2015. "Digital Technologies and the Global Economy's Productivity Imperative." McKinsey Global Institute, Paris and San Francisco. *Digiworld Economic Journal* 100(4): 47–64.
Lemaire, Axelle. 2016. Forging a Digital Society OECD Yearbook. http://www.oecdobserver.org/news/fullstory.php/aid/5579/Forging_a_digital_society.html#sthash.OHfIHWOG.dpuf
McGee, Suzanne. 2016. How the Gig Economy Is Helping Make the Case for Universal Basic Income. *The Guardian*, June 9, sec. US news. https://www.theguardian.com/us-news/us-money-blog/2016/jun/09/universal-basic-income-gig-economy-technology
Mescoli, Felix. 2016. dm-Gründer fordert 1.000 Euro monatlich für jeden—seine Begründung ist verdammt gut. *Business Insider*, Wirtschaft sec. June 10. http://www.businessinsider.de/dm-gruender-goetz-werner-grundeinkommen-befeuert-das-spiel-wie-beim-monopoly-2016-6?IR=T
Mesthene, Emmanuel G. 1968. How Technology Will Shape the Future. *Science* 161(3837): 135–142. http://science.sciencemag.org/content/161/3837/135. doi:10.1126/science.161.3837.135
Metz, Cade. 2015. Robots Will Steal Our Jobs, But They'll Give Us New Ones. *Wired*, August 24. http://www.wired.com/2015/08/robots-will-steal-jobs-theyll-give-us-new-ones/
Mokyr, Joel, Chris Vickers, and Nicolas L. Ziebarth. 2015. The History of Technological Anxiety and the Future of Economic Growth: Is This Time Different? *Journal of Economic Perspectives*. 29(3): 31–50.

Nevis, Seamus. 2016. Lifelong Learning: Reforming Education for an Age of Technological and Demographic Change. Institute of Directors Policy Report, March.http://www.iod.com/influencing/press-office/press-releases/business-leaders-launch-action-plan-for-education-in-the-age-of-automation

OECD. 2015. *Education at a Glance 2015: OECD Indicators.* Paris: OECD Publishing. http://dx.doi.org/10.1787/eag-2015-en

———. 2016. *Labour and Employment Ministerial Meeting, Building More Resilient and Inclusive Labour Markets.* Paris, January. http://www.oecd.org/employment/ministerial/policy-forum/

Oxfam International. Briefing Paper. 2016. *An Economy for the 1%: How Privilege and Power in the Economy Drive Extreme Inequality and How This Can be Stopped.* Oxfam, January. https://www.oxfam.org/en/research/economy-1

Peterson, Ryan. 2016. The Driverless Truck is Coming, and It's Going to Automate Millions of Jobs. *TechCrunch.* https://techcrunch.com/2016/04/25/the-driverless-truck-is-coming-and-its-going-to-automate-millions-ofjobs/

Rotman, David. 2013. How Technology Is Destroying Jobs. *MIT Technology Review,* June 12. https://www.technologyreview.com/s/515926/how-technology-is-destroying-jobs/

———. 2015. Who Will Own the Robots? *MIT Technology Review,* June 16. https://www.technologyreview.com/s/538401/who-will-own-the-robots/

Smith, Aaron, and Janna Anderson. 2014. *AI, Robotics, and the Future of Jobs.* Pew Research Center, August. http://www.pewinternet.org/2014/08/06/future-of-jobs/

Stefan Hajkowicz, Andrew Reeson, Lachlan Rudd, Alexandra Bratanova, Leonie Hodgers, Claire Mason, and Naomi Boughen. January. http://www.data61.csiro.au/~/media/D61/Files/16-0026_DATA61_REPORT_TomorrowsDigiallyEnabledWorkforce_WEB_160204.pdf

Summers, Lawrence H. 2014. Lawrence H. Summers on the Economic Challenge of the Future: Jobs. *Wall Street Journal,* July 7. http://www.wsj.com/articles/lawrence-h-summers-on-the-economic-challenge-of-the-future-jobs-1404762501

Talwar, Rohit and Tim Hancock. 2010. *The Shape of Jobs to Come: Possible New Careers Emerging from Advances in Science and Technology (2010–2030).* Fast Future Research, January. http://fastfuture.com/wp-content/uploads/2010/01/FastFuture_Shapeofjobstocome_FullReport1.pdf

The Washington Post. 2010. The Lost Decade for the Economy. Business sec. January. http://www.washingtonpost.com/wp-dyn/content/graphic/2010/01/01/GR2010010101478.html

Thompson, Derek. 2015. A World Without Work. *The Atlantic,* July/August Issue.http://www.theatlantic.com/magazine/archive/2015/07/world-without-work/395294/

Thomson, Stephanie. 2016. GDP a Poor Measure of Progress, Say Davos Economists. *World Economic Forum*. Agenda sec. January 23. https://www.weforum.org/agenda/2016/01/gdp

United Nations Department of Economic and Social Affairs. 2013. Assessing the Future of Employment. November 11. http://www.un.org/en/development/desa/news/ecosoc/future-of-employment.html

United Nations. Department of Economic and Social Affairs, Population Division. 2015. *World Population Prospects: The 2015 Revision, Key Findings and Advance Tables*. Working Paper No. ESA/P/WP.241. https://esa.un.org/unpd/wpp/publications/files/key_findings_wpp_2015.pdf

United Nations. Economic and Social Council and the Economic and Financial Committee (Second Committee) of the General Assembly Special Joint Meeting. 2013. *The Future of Employment: The World of Work in 2030*. http://www.un.org/en/ga/second/68/employment.pdf

US Department of Labor. Bureau of Labor Statistics Release. 2015. *Employment Projections: 2014–2024*. USDL-15-2327. December 8. http://www.bls.gov/news.release/pdf/ecopro.pdf

US News & World Report. 2016. US News Best Jobs Rankings. http://money.usnews.com/careers/best-jobs/personal-care-aide/salary

van Parijs, Philippe. 2016. The Worldwide March to Basic Income: Thank You Switzerland! June 6. http://www.basicincome.org/news/2016/06/the-worldwide-march-to-basic-income-thank-you-switzerland/

Wallach, Wendell, and Gary Marchant. 2015. Coordinating Technological Governance. *Issues in Science and Technology* 31(4): 43–49. http://issues.org/31-4/coordinating-technology-governance/

Wallis, Stewart. 2016. Five Measures of Growth that Are Better than GDP. *World Economic Forum*. Agenda sec. April 19. https://www.weforum.org/agenda/2016/04/five-measures-of-growth-that-are-better-than-gdp

Watts, Martin. 2002. Basic Income: A Review of the Issues. *New Zealand Journal of Industrial Relations* 27(1): 119–133.

Wohlson, Marcus. 2014. When Robots Take All the Work, What'll Be Left for Us to Do? *Wired*. https://www.wired.com/2014/08/when-robots-take-all-the-work-whatll-be-left-for-us-to-do/

World Economic Forum. 2016. *The Future of Jobs: Employment, Skills and Workforce Strategy for the Fourth Industrial Revolution*, Geneva. http://reports.weforum.org/future-of-jobs-2016/

CHAPTER 7

Unconditional Basic Income as a Solution to Technological Unemployment

Scott Santens

In the opening of the film *2001: A Space Odyssey*, viewers are shown a historic moment in time where primitive man used the first tool. It was a bone, and when used like a club, it allowed a physically weaker group to overpower a physically stronger group. The story is, of course, fictional, but at some point in time we as humans did use our first tool, and ever since that day, directly because of our tool usage, we as a species have been able to accomplish increasingly more with increasingly less. Buckminster Fuller referred to this process as "ephemeralization." The theoretical endpoint of this process exists as an asymptote that we can only approach but never reach, where we gain the ability to accomplish everything with nothing. This should sound great. It is. But there's a catch. There's always a catch.

WHAT'S THE CATCH?

The catch is of our own making. The catch, and it's a big one, is twofold. First, we require the exchange of money for the basic necessities of life like food and shelter. And second, we require the exchange of work in order to obtain money. The result of this pairing is that we systematically require

S. Santens (✉)
USBIG, Inc., New Orleans, LA, USA
e-mail: scott@scottsantens.com

© The Author(s) 2017
K. LaGrandeur, J.J. Hughes (eds.), *Surviving the Machine Age*,
DOI 10.1007/978-3-319-51165-8_7

the exchange of work to stay alive. So as long as everyone can exchange their labor for income, moral issues of involuntary servitude aside, everyone can then theoretically survive in a system where private property is established and enforced. However, tool use throws an unavoidable wrench into this system.

That Wrench Is Technological Unemployment

The ability to find paid work is rooted within supply and demand. If there is a demand for your labor, and few can supply it in the same way you do, you will do well. If many can supply it just like you, you may not do so well, but you may also manage to get by if you're lucky. However, we've been busy building tools far beyond those made out of bone, and these newer tools are increasingly able to meet our demand for labor without any need for us. So the question becomes, if machines can supply the demand for labor, and at a lower price point, what happens to the ability of living human beings to work, and therefore to live, and even to obtain what all the machines are producing?

There can only be three solutions to this self-created conundrum based on our twofold catch. We can either stop requiring the exchange of money for basic needs, essentially making certain things like food, water, and shelter entirely free. Or we can guarantee that everyone can always find paid work for enough income to exchange for the fulfillment of basic needs. Or we can stop requiring the exchange of work for money by paying everyone an income whether they work or not, and the amount would just need to be sufficient enough to cover basic needs.

The first option would destroy the price system for basic goods and services. This would in turn destroy the ability to calculate just what to produce, how much of it to produce, and where it's needed. This option is a command economy or planned economy for basic goods and services. The second would guarantee that in a world of machines being able to do an increasing amount of work better than us humans, the work we could guarantee to ourselves would be increasingly pointless—the equivalent of digging holes and filling them. This is the job guarantee (JG). The third would fully preserve the price system and entirely avoid the pitfalls of unnecessary work. In fact, it would not only preserve the price system, but also enhance it, and it would not only avoid the creation of unnecessary work, it would also reduce it. That third option is the unconditional basic income (UBI).

If technological unemployment is the Gordian knot of the twenty-first century, basic income is the sword that cuts through it. By simply severing the connection between income and work through the unconditional provision of an income for life always sufficient for basic needs, the fear of technological unemployment is removed. It doesn't stop there though, because the right to a basic income has repercussions beyond the removal of fear, and these repercussions are themselves systemically transformative.

To understand just how transformative basic income thus stands to be, we must first more closely examine the full magnitude of technological unemployment as something that is not a problem that exists in the future, but one that is already here. To claim everyone is just crying wolf is false. Sheep are actively being eaten as we speak. We just don't choose to see it. Then we must look at the economic system we've created with new eyes to see the core problem that's been with us for so long we accept it as normal, and that's the inability of anyone without sufficient property to say no to working for those who own most of it. And finally we must come to recognize our interdependence within an economic system where our growing productivity is our common heritage, and thus our common wealth no one person or group can claim a monopoly to. As productivity grows with ongoing automation, so too should the basic income grow as a kind of prosperity dividend. What is at first basic should eventually be the right of every citizen shareholder to the vast wealth of an automated nation.

THE INVISIBLE SHEEP

Warnings of oncoming technological unemployment have been with us for over a century. Over and over again someone has called attention to the ability of capital in the form of machines to replace labor in the form of humans. This fear has been expressed so often, people refer to it as the Luddite Fallacy. It's actively considered fallacious to point out the very real potential that machines can do the work of humans to the point that human labor sees as much demand as horse labor after the introduction of cars. And so here we are today, where very smart people are looking around at all the jobs that still exist and are actively being created, and then claiming it as evidence in support of a perceived fantasy of technological unemployment. The thing is, we aren't looking closely enough at the jobs we have, because we need jobs, and thus it's in our own interest to not look closely enough. Never underestimate the unwillingness of someone to see the reality, if their lives depend on seeing a fantasy.

The invention of the computer did indeed change forever the way we work. Beginning in the 1970s, we have been eliminating jobs involving a medium amount of skill (Autor 2015)—consider, for instance, manufacturing as we replaced car assembly line workers with robots. And what jobs we couldn't automate, we used our new technologies to pack up and ship offshore to places like China and India where labor was cheaper. In place of those jobs that made up the heart of the middle-class, we created and grew the service industry in its place. For decades we've created more and more low-skill jobs—think fast food restaurants—to fill the holes in the labor market cored out by technology. Since 1990, even the growth of jobs defined as involving routine tasks has ended (Dvorkin 2016). More than that, because not having a job and simultaneously not being impoverished is something we've never really allowed as a real choice, we've perpetuated and even created jobs that need not exist. In an article for *Strike! Magazine* in August of 2013, David Graeber refers to this kind of employment as "bullshit jobs," for example, lobbyists and telemarketers, as opposed to actually important work like refuse collection and nursing. This is what's likely behind the huge percentages of people all over the world who don't feel engaged or even feel actively disengaged from their jobs—estimated at 87% (Crabtree 2013). People are increasingly spending their days in many jobs where they are not actually working, plastered instead to their social network feeds and smartphones. People are clocking in 47 hours of work a week (Saad 2014) in jobs that require only 40 and often only working for only 25–30 hours. This is a huge drag on productivity and a monumental waste of human potential.

Meanwhile, it's more than just the binary situation of job or no job. Jobs themselves have been in the process of transforming from full-time decades-long careers to a series of non–full-time alternative jobs that are bounced among in terms of years, months, and even hours instead of decades. This century alone something new has taken over, and that's the growth of these forms of alternative work where people are no longer really considered employees but alternative workers. Such alternative work is in the form of temp agency workers, on-call workers, independent contractors, and freelancers. Some call it the 1099 economy, short for the different form required by the Internal Revenue Service (IRS) at tax time for "non-employees." In fact, since 2005, all nine million net newly created jobs are in this sector (Katz and Krueger 2016). It's the rise of short-term employment and self-employment where employee benefits and rights have gone by the wayside, and though many love the greater sense of autonomy, a greater sense of insecurity comes right along with it. Even more recently, the gig economy has been born, where self-employment has been taskified, and it's up to everyone to patch together sufficient income on a daily basis, never knowing for sure if they'll be able to cover the rent like they once could with a long-term, steady paycheck.

All the above is the invisible flock of sheep being eaten one by one as we turn our heads away and claim technological unemployment is a fantasy. Technological unemployment cannot exist in the way we've always feared, where no new jobs are created as a result of elimination, as long as we require the existence of jobs. We will instead fill that hole with useless jobs, and jobs ripe for replacement as soon as the technology becomes cheaper than the cost of desperate workers willing to work for handfuls of pocket change in order to get by. Technological unemployment is so much more than actual unemployment. Because technology allows the greater granularity of breaking jobs into tasks—taskification—another facet of technological unemployment is technological underemployment. In other words, it's not just about automation, it's about *atomization*.

Meanwhile our existing safety nets are not built to handle such realities. It's one thing to, maybe once in a lifetime, need to meet with a program administrator and jump through their hoops for financial assistance. It's entirely another for bureaucracy to become a perpetual fact of life, where you never know if you'll meet the requirements, and you must make the decision of whether taking that part-time job or gig as an Uber driver is even worth it if you're going to lose your benefits and be faced with the possibility of trying to jump through all those hoops all over again. Our safety nets are not built for flexibility. What we need is a firm floor that lies underneath everyone and requires no bureaucracy. It would always be there. It would be under full-timers. It would be under part-timers. It would be under sub-contractors. It would be underneath everyone in the gig economy. It would even be under would-be entrepreneurs. Unconditional basic income would be such a bureaucracy-free universal floor built for maximum flexibility.

The time to prepare ourselves for the future was yesterday. The effects of technology are not around the corner. They're in our past, and they're here right now. And it's directly because we've never instituted basic income, and in so doing made working fully voluntary, that we've not allowed our jobs to disappear without replacement. The boy cried wolf, and the boy was right. We just happen to have created a world where seeing dead sheep is considered delusional, when really the world where we create useless work and look the other way as inequality grows and economic security shrinks is what's truly delusional. The granting of a basic income will release us all from this collective delusion.

THE MISSING RIGHT

What lies at the heart of the invisible sheep problem is our inability to say no to jobs. Without that power, we are effectively enslaved. To live we must eat. To eat we must have money. To have money we must sell our labor. There is no real option to just live off the land with our own sweat because all the land is owned. And so we must toil for those who own land. There is no other name for that but slavery, but we don't call it that. Instead we call it the labor market. But anyone interested in free markets must care about free people within those markets, and the only way for people to be free is to be granted the right of refusal to work for others.

Once one understands how important the right of refusal is, much more comes into focus. There can be no individual bargaining power without the right to refuse. Being able to walk away means being able to negotiate the true value of human labor. If human labor were thus priced accurately in a free labor market, low demand jobs would be rewarded more because fewer people would be willing to do them unless paid sufficiently, and where the cost of human labor becomes higher than the cost of automation, machines can be welcomed to fill that job. Think of garbage collectors. If no one wanted to do that work for $30,000 per year because they already have a basic income of $12,000 per year, an offer of $100,000 per year in additional income would attract many to do that job. If the cost of automating that job is the equivalent of $90,000 per year, automation is the cheaper option and no one need do that job anymore. The result is the complete transformation of a social system built around a goal of full employment, where everyone has a job, to a new goal of full unemployment where as many jobs as possible are offloaded to machines, granting people the ability to pursue whatever is most important to them as living breathing humans with limited lifespans.

The right to refuse is even so important it lies underneath all other rights. Do you really have the right to free speech as long as you're afraid of being fired? How many times have you wanted to say something, and decided against it, just in case? When was the last time you considered taking to the streets in an act of civil disobedience, but feared the repercussions to your present and future employment? How many times has someone somewhere not voted out of fear they'd be late for their job, and potentially lose it? For those who most value the right to bear arms, do you really have that right if you can't afford to purchase the arms? To what else can that be applied? How many things in life do we think of as basic rights that don't truly exist due to lack of money or fear of economic destitution?

Arguably, it's the right to a basic income that makes all other rights actually possible. People become free to speak their minds with the fear of destitution off the table. People become free to march in the streets and to get to work late because voting was more important. With a guarantee of economic security, all other rights are empowered. Without the recognition of economic rights, all other rights are infringed. Basic income is our missing economic right, from which our other incomplete rights become complete.

Finally achieving the ability to say "No" after the adoption of basic income, changes the rules of the game entirely. It represents the dawn of recognition that any advanced society should pursue not full employment, but full unemployment. Society prospers when every member within it is fully free to prosper.

THE RETURN OF THE COMMON WEALTH

No one person can claim 100% ownership of their wealth. It's all fractions of the whole. As the saying goes, no one person can make a pencil. As simple a creation as that seems, it is the collective work of humanity. The wood comes from somewhere. The graphite comes from somewhere else. The eraser and what comprises it come from elsewhere. Shipping networks transport raw materials that are made into component parts that are manufactured into a finished product that is shipped all over the world. More than that, no one alive thought of the pencil. That person is long dead.

We all prosper because of knowledge from the past, passed down to us. This is our collective "something for nothing" we all enjoy on the one hand, while deriding the idea of something for nothing on the other. Civilization itself is something for nothing. It is the result of billions of interdependent parts working together as part of a social system known as humanity.

Land value too is its own clear example of wealth created collectively. When something we own goes up in value as the result of our doing nothing, that added value is the result of everything and everyone around the land, not anything we ourselves did. Similarly, transport a piece of high-priced metropolitan land into the middle of nowhere, with no one else around, no resources, no infrastructure, no nothing, and the value of the land becomes nothing. It should be clear that the increasing value of land should be shared with the ones creating the value, which is *everyone*.

Advancing technology is also common wealth, the result of those today standing on the shoulders of the giants of the past. Additionally, it's even the result of tax dollars being invested into the public research and development that makes all the advancements possible. The iPhone wasn't created in a vacuum by Apple. It was built on the technologies pioneered by government-funded research (Mazzucato 2015). Big data aren't created in a vacuum either. It is the result of our collective interactions. It is the mining of natural resources where the mines are each and every one of us, and the ore is the information we all create through our interactions with each other.

We are completely surrounded by uncompensated commonly created wealth. Now, this isn't to say that 100% of all wealth should be shared among all equally. It's simply the recognition that a fraction of all wealth should be justly shared with everyone, because that fraction is created by everyone. And as productivity continues to grow, as our society continues to achieve more and more with less and less—Fuller's ephemeralization process—that productivity should be recognized as the shared creation it is and compensated appropriately.

This is where basic income becomes more than basic income. The idea of a basic income is simply the starting point. It is the recognition that, at the very least, our collective wealth creation and our right to say no to each other in a technologically advancing world should be met with an absolute minimum of sufficient access to resources to have all our basic needs met. And as technology continues to advance and productivity continues to grow, our unconditional access to all resources should grow as well because we are all in some way contributing to all of it. In ways impossible to measure, we interdependently grow our collective prosperity, and it should be recognized with a growing dividend—a prosperity dividend—universally provided without condition.

As prosperity continues to grow, the eventual endpoint of basic income is thus an amount of access to resources that can only be considered effectively infinite. By effectively infinite, I mean the ongoing process of ephemeralization through advancing technology will allow the meeting of wants and needs with fewer and fewer resources. Whereas 20% of a

$20 trillion economy is $4 trillion, 20% of a $200 trillion economy is $40 trillion, which is the difference between a $12,000 per year basic income and a $120,000 per year prosperity dividend. The higher the minimum amount, and the cheaper the goods and services possible to spend it on, the harder it is to spend all of it, and therefore it increasingly becomes effectively infinite. When everyone receives as a minimum, an amount of access to resources that goes so far that most people find it difficult to ever actually "spend," money itself loses meaning. The result is something more like an economy based on resources instead of money, where what is possible is measured by if we can physically achieve it instead of if we can "afford" it. Some may call this post-capitalism. Others may call it a Star Trek economy. Still others may call it a resource-based economy. But it doesn't really matter what we call it, because it lies beyond, and only if we make that first all important step together—unconditional income.

The connection between work and income must be severed. That Gordian knot of our own creation must be undone. Our growing insecurity must be ended. Our inability to say no must be abolished. And our interdependent creation of our thus far uncompensated common wealth building must be compensated.

An unconditional basic income achieves all of those things. It is far more than what some see as "a few crumbs" tossed to the great masses as compensation for technological unemployment. It is the abolition of enslavement once and for all, and the beginning of a new kind of society built on higher achievements of purpose than toil for paychecks. It is the destiny of a species that picked up its first tool and imagined a way to use it to achieve all that could not otherwise be achieved without.

Is basic income a sufficient response to technological unemployment? It's more than that. It's the most important response of all. It is a collective step that is humanity's next giant leap.

REFERENCES

Autor, David H. 2015. Why Are There Still So Many Jobs? The History and Future of Workplace Automation. *Journal of Economic Perspectives* 29(3): 3–30. doi:10.1257/jep.29.3.3.

Crabtree, Steve. 2013. Worldwide, 13% of Employees Are Engaged at Work. *Gallup*, October 8. http://www.gallup.com/poll/165269/worldwide-employees-engaged-work.aspx

Dvorkin, Maximiliano. 2016. Jobs Involving Routine Tasks Aren't Growing. Federal Reserve Bank of St. Louis, January 4. https://www.stlouisfed.org/on-the-economy/2016/january/jobs-involving-routine-tasks-arent-growing

Katz, Lawrence F., and Alan B. Krueger. 2016. The Rise and Nature of Alternative Work Arrangements in the United States, 1995–2015. Working Paper, March 29. http://krueger.princeton.edu/sites/default/files/akrueger/files/katz_krueger_cws_-_march_29_20165.pdf

Mazzucato, Mariana. 2015. *The Entrepreneurial State: Debunking Public vs Private Sector Myths*. New York: Anthem Press.

Saad, Lydia. 2014. The "40-Hour" Workweek Is Actually Longer—By Seven Hours. *Gallup*, August 29. http://www.gallup.com/poll/175286/hour-workweek-actually-longer-seven-hours.aspx

CHAPTER 8

Policy Solutions to Technological Unemployment

Yvonne A. Stevens and Gary E. Marchant

INTRODUCTION

Computers, automated systems, artificial intelligence, and robots are replacing human jobs. It is a matter of empirical debate how many jobs are being lost, and whether new jobs created by these emerging technologies approach the number of jobs lost, both now and in the future. Regardless of the answer to this critical question, which remains unknown and unknowable at the present time, there is a serious risk, if not a factual certainty, that increasing numbers of workers will be replaced by machines in the foreseeable future. As such, it is important to explore potential policy options to address the impending challenge of technological unemployment before it creates misery and despair for untold numbers of dislocated workers and renders permanent and irreversible tears in the social fabric.

The most common proposed policy response to the technological unemployment problem is some form of a basic guaranteed income. This option is addressed more fully elsewhere in this volume. While the basic guaranteed income has a strong moral and practical underpinning, we do not advocate

Y.A. Stevens (✉) • G.E. Marchant
Sandra Day O'Connor College of Law, Arizona State University,
Phoenix, AZ, USA
e-mail: ystevens@asu.edu; Gary.Marchant@asu.edu

© The Author(s) 2017   117
K. LaGrandeur, J.J. Hughes (eds.), *Surviving the Machine Age*,
DOI 10.1007/978-3-319-51165-8_8

such an approach, on its own or as typically formulated, for reasons we have elaborated previously (Marchant et al. 2014). Briefly, a guaranteed national income that gives recipients an automatic monthly check fails to provide an incentive to find work or engage in other meaningful and beneficial activities. At the same time, it provides an automatic government handout to individuals while reducing their esteem in their own eyes and those of their neighbors and contacts. A guaranteed income program that provides a monthly check to every adult in the country (including those who do not need it) would be very expensive and wasteful, yet limiting the checks to the unemployed creates an even stronger disincentive to employment.

There may be ways to restructure the general concept of the basic guaranteed income to address these problems of incentives, stigma, and self-esteem, and we explore our favored long-term solution in the final half of this paper, where we support and elaborate on a "Badge" proposal. But before getting there, we first identify and critically evaluate a number of other incremental policy proposals, both good and bad, feasible and effective or not. Of course, none of these proposed solutions is exclusive, so it may be that a portfolio of such policy interventions will be needed to best address the problem of technological unemployment.

INCREMENTAL SOLUTIONS

Mandating Employment

The simplest way to protect jobs is to mandate employment, either directly through legislation or indirectly through labor agreements. For example, the States of New Jersey and Oregon prohibit drivers from pumping their own gasoline at service stations, a requirement initially adopted in 1949 in New Jersey and 1951 in Oregon to protect public safety, but which now functions primarily to protect gas attendant jobs, although Oregon recently eased certain restrictions (Sullivan 2014). Similarly, labor laws in Japan prohibited employers from laying off workers, resulting in employees who were no longer needed being placed in a "chasing-out room" or "boredom room" where they would do nothing but play cards and read newspapers all day while collecting their guaranteed paychecks (Tabuchi 2013). Similarly, some companies in France assign workers who are no longer needed but who have long-term job security to the dreaded "le placard" (the closet) where they try to make workplace conditions so miserable that the employee will quit his or her job (Druckerman 2016). Protecting jobs that might otherwise be lost as a result of rapid technological innovation makes sense in a backward-thinking economy. But it is a costly solution in terms of impeding innovation, competiveness, and efficiency—any nation that attempts to implement such a policy runs the risk of being left behind competitively. Job protectionist policies may therefore provide some short-term benefits in protecting some jobs, but fail to address the underlying pressures that reduce demand for employment, and increase inefficiencies that are unlikely to be sustainable in the long-run (Dau-Schmidt 2001).

Government Job Creation

A long-standing strategy is for government to fund or subsidize jobs directly. From President Franklin D. Roosevelt's Works Progress Administration to the Peace Corps and the military, government-created jobs have helped to fill in employment gaps in the private sector and provide meaningful work to otherwise unemployed workers. There are many needs and opportunities that government funding could address in a beneficial way while also creating jobs, from infrastructure restoration, to environmental cleanup and urban renewal, to care-giving and assistance for the elderly and ill people. Of course, such activities would require significant government funding, but providing jobs for these worthwhile activities may have important benefits for the individual and society relative to a guaranteed annual income for recipients doing nothing beneficial. One option would be an "employer of last resort" program in which the government would provide jobs at the federal minimum wage (plus benefits) for anyone willing to work diligently on socially beneficial assignments (Wray 2011).

Work Sharing

Another set of strategies seeks to share the available work among more workers, such as by reducing the number of hours an individual employee works per day, week, or year. The logic is simple—if there is less total human work to be done, spread that work over a greater number of workers by reducing the number of hours worked per employee. Some Silicon Valley employers have experimented with shorter work weeks, with some favorable results (Tracy 2013; Ebdrup 2013). While these ideas may succeed in providing meaningful work to a greater number of human workers, their obvious weakness is that the compensation per worker may also decrease, unless supplemented by private or governmental subsidies. These strategies therefore help divide the pie more evenly, but do not grow the size of the pie (Vardi 2012).

Employment Impact Statements

Another indirect strategy for promoting employment is to require greater awareness and attention to the employment impacts of legislative and regulatory actions. This requirement could be based on the environmental impact statements required for major federal actions under the National Environmental Policy Act. For example, an employment impact statement could be required for all new legislative and regulatory enactments at the federal and state levels that would project employment impacts of the proposed new law. The comparative employment impacts of alternatives to the proposed enactment could also be required. Such a procedural step would not directly protect jobs, but would facilitate greater awareness by policymakers of the employment impacts of their actions, and possible alternatives.

Educational and Training Reforms

Although educational and training reforms are discussed in more detail elsewhere in this volume, this topic is briefly mentioned here given its critical importance to mitigating technological employment. Many high-technology and skilled job positions are currently going unfilled because our twentieth-century education system is not providing the dynamic and updated training necessary to fill those positions (Bessen 2015). The old model of concentrating education and training into the first quarter-century of life must shift to a life-long training paradigm in which workers are continuously being trained and updated to match new employment opportunities and technologies. For example, the ACT Foundation has envisioned a future lifelong learning system called the Learning Ledger, which keeps an account of each individual's educational and learning credits achieved throughout their lives, with educational units available from a wide variety of institutions and organizations (ACT Foundation 2016).

Tax Policy and Financial Incentives

Tax policy and other government financial incentives could be used to promote job creation. For example, a tax credit could be provided for each new job provided, creating an incentive for an employer to favor a human over machine worker in marginal cases. Tax policy incentives could also be targeted at employees rather than just employers, such as by,

POLICY SOLUTIONS TO TECHNOLOGICAL UNEMPLOYMENT   121

for example, expanding the earned income tax credit (EITC) to provide greater rewards for individuals on government support to add to their income by taking on new jobs.

Small Business Incentives

Small business is an important generator of jobs—accounting for 60% of all new jobs in the United States over a recent 15-year period (U.S. White House 2011). In addition to the number of jobs, small businesses are important for addressing technological unemployment because laid off workers with relevant skills and ideas can start their own small businesses, allowing for a self-help solution rather than relying on an existing large employer to hire them for limited or non-existent jobs. Therefore, policy options that incentivize or facilitate individuals to start their own small business could be important generators of new employment. Potential policies for stimulating new small business creation include subsidies, tax incentives, educational and training programs for start-ups, and government purchase preferences.

Support for New Job Paradigms

Yet another engine of potential job growth in the era of technological unemployment is likely to be the "gig economy," in which growing numbers of people support themselves economically through a set of limited-duration and part-time compensated undertakings, or "gigs" (Harris and Krueger 2015). Instead of deriving all their income from a single full-time job, participants in the gig economy collect revenues from a variety of sources, which may include some part-time or occasional work in a traditional job like waiter, perhaps some contract work, some participation in the sharing economy (e.g., Uber driver or Airbnb host), and maybe some creative activities such as art or handicrafts that are sold. While not providing the same level and stability of revenue as a traditional job, the gig economy is expected to provide a livelihood for an increasing share of the population, many of whom enjoy the increased flexibility and freedom associated with that type of livelihood. To help maximize the quantity and quality of the gig economy, policymakers should modernize obsolete and outdated job classification and employment policies to better enable and empower workers in the gig economy (Kennedy 2016). For example, one impediment to the gig economy is that healthcare has traditionally been linked to traditional employment, tying workers to full-time employers and jobs. This structure for healthcare may no longer make sense—healthcare benefits should be freed from the workplace just as car insurance or housing payments are. Others have suggested the creation of an office for inter-generational responsibility to help assess policies that would affect younger workers who tend to be clustered in the gig economy (Furchtgott-Roth 2015).

Technological Innovation

Finally, even though technological innovation (particularly in the computer, robot, and AI fields) is the driver of technological unemployment, many types of technological innovation are continuing to generate new jobs. For example, personalized medicine is greatly increasing demand for genetic counselors, drones are creating thousands of new jobs for designers and operators, 3D printers are creating brand new markets for CAD files, and artificial intelligence is creating strong demand for coders and software engineers. While some have suggested that the threat of technological unemployment might justify slowing technological innovation, such an approach would not only deny society the benefits of new technologies, but would also likely do more harm than good with respect to employment opportunities. We need smarter innovation, which, in part, is directed at creating valuable new job and career opportunities.

A LONG-TERM SOLUTION: THE BADGE PROPOSAL

Our longer-term policy option attempts to alter the existing social model in which a person's economic livelihood, social status, and personal self-worth are rooted in employment. We instead propose the development of an alternative and broader system of social reward and credit, which we refer to as the "Badge" concept.

Society is currently structured in such a way that people work for themselves or an employer and are remunerated for their efforts with money. This money, in turn, is saved, invested, or converted into goods and services that are deemed necessary or are otherwise valuable to the income-earner. Some have theorized that this economic model may, in the near future, no longer be viable as technology takes away jobs previously held by human workers (e.g., Ford 2009). With increasingly fewer jobs available, former workers will no longer earn the money necessary to purchase goods, services, and housing costs. If this opportunity is lost, a new social system may be required to satisfy human necessities and desires, as well as to sustain a consumer market to buy or otherwise receive the products and services others develop and sell. The new model will also likely be necessary to preserve and foster human dignity, respect, and accomplishment, something that, for many, is gained through daily work. Contributions to society, in the form of paid work or volunteering, generally enhance and promote a psychologically healthy, meaningful life.

Should the feared advent of technological unemployment come to be realized, many individuals will likely be required to seek and find personal satisfaction outside of the employment context. The activities undertaken to gain fulfillment will vary and may consist of caregiving activities, artistry, creative inventions, good deeds, and other socially valuable contributions. These worthy contributions may require incentives and rewards. We previously theorized that "simply giving handouts to affected persons undercuts their respect to both themselves and the members of their community" and would appear to have a negative impact on motivation (Marchant et al. 2014, p. 39).

The incentives themselves could be applied, as needed, to amenities such as shelter, food, clothing, healthcare, and so forth that are necessary to live a full and satisfactory life. Nonetheless, it may be that such a reward system may be better suited to *supplemental* goods and services that are desired but not necessary for basic living. This would be the case where money, as a valued means of exchange, is still in circulation, for example, as a basic income, provided by the government to meet basic needs. It would also be the case if, due to increased productivity as a result of technology, basic goods and services are free to all citizens due to abundance and economic availability, potentially resulting in money's loss as a valued or necessary means of exchange. This model is similar to a resource-based economy where technology would be used,

> To overcome some scarce resources by applying renewable sources of energy, computerizing and automating manufacturing and inventory, designing safe energy-efficient cities and advanced transportation systems, providing universal healthcare and more relevant education, and most of all by generating a new incentive system based on human and environmental concern. (The Venus Project 2016)

In a resource-based economy, goods and services are made available to all individuals without the need for a monetary exchange system. However, one could add a step to this or a similar model, whereby while individuals would have their basic needs met, they would be motivated by a separate, supplemental reward system that could provide a way to trade the reward for a desire or simply for the recognition of having made a worthy contribution.

If, as some have suggested, money is no longer in circulation due to it having lost its value and use in this new era of technological unemployment, then the novel reward system could, conceptually, be used to "purchase" *both* basics and extras. The problem with this proposal is, of course, that money, as a tangible "thing," could just as easily remain in circulation as the representative reward system for socially valuable contributions. Why replace money with a different element if it is accomplishing the same end? The alternative valuation model, therefore, appears to work best as a *supplement* to meeting the most basic needs.

Naturally, the new reward model would need to be valued by society. The value attributed to money by society, as a collective, is why money has thrived as a common medium of exchange. In essence, "the value of money essentially depends on people believing in it," and belief can fade, making the transition to an alternative system feasible (Asmundson and Oner 2012). For instance, China, the first country to use paper bills during the Tang Dynasty, at one point eliminated the practice as a result of inflation in 1455 and did not resume use of paper money for hundreds of years. Generally speaking, eliminating money from an automated workforce society might maximize individual contributions to the betterment of human and environmental health as a whole. People might be in a position to no longer involve themselves in unfulfilling activities in which they previously engaged in for the sake of a paycheck. Giving individuals the opportunity to choose which activities provide the greatest fulfillment while at the same time contributing to society would result in a happier and healthier existence for all.

The Badge system proposed here would provide an alternative "currency" for measuring and rewarding an individual's beneficial contribution to society. While some have suggested that a return to a barter system could be used to replace or supplement the existing money-based economy, the badge proposal is much broader than a barter system. While a barter system is focused on the exchange of private goods or services between individuals, the Badge system rewards broader contributions beyond private goods to also value public goods such as, for example, producing open source software, creating public works of art, or providing environmental clean-up. Moreover, there would be some private benefits, such as helping an ailing and poor person who cannot afford to provide compensation in financial or in-kind services. Finally, a barter system is often challenged by the lack of an appropriate commodity to barter (what if no one wants what I have?), and the lack of a common measure of value.

How then would a Badge system reward meaningful and beneficial contributions to society? There has been quite a bit written about the theory of motivation with regard to rewards and the power of incentives. Some, like Dan Pink, espouse the view that while rewards work in some instances, they do not work in others (Pink 2009). Basing this opinion on several studies, Pink claims that the carrot-or-stick approach does not work when it comes to what he calls "twenty-first century tasks." Twenty-first century tasks involve creative problem-solving and are opposite to rule-based tasks. They are the kinds of tasks that as of yet, do not lend themselves very well to automation. Pink notes that, among other completed studies, London School of Economics researchers considered 51 studies and found that "financial incentives can result in a negative impact on overall performance" (Pink 2009). Pink relies on the concept of intrinsic motivation, which is "the desire to do things because they matter, because we like it, they're interesting or part of something important" and "that new operating system...revolves around three elements: autonomy, mastery and purpose." He then provides examples that when individuals are given the opportunity to work on anything they desire, without reward, for fun, they are much more motivated and productive, and he cites Google and Wikipedia as examples (Pink 2009).

Therefore, perhaps a new valuation model is not even required. If rewards do not matter and might actually make things worse, then why bother? If and when technological unemployment occurs might we be better off not providing incentives to motivate people to accomplish more? Not necessarily. Recognition is one of the key factors that promotes intrinsic motivation whereby learners feel satisfaction when others recognize and appreciate their accomplishments (P2P Foundation 2015). Additionally, not all social scientists agree with Pink. Gerry Ledford, a senior research scientist at the University of Southern California, believes scientific studies establish just the opposite. Ledford claims that a review of 43 field studies illustrated that intrinsic motivation is increased by external incentives and that incentives typically result in better performance

(Ledford 2013). Within the context of technological unemployment, author Martin Ford and other have suggested an incentive-based framework whereby incentives,

> ... [i]f fulfilled, would have a positive effect on one's income: the greater the response to the incentives, the greater the income the individual will receive. Such incentives might include participation in environmental stewardship, continuing education, child-care, art, music, volunteer work and other laudable activities. Ford's proposal arguably eliminates the often negative effects of having "idle hands," low self-esteem associated with job loss, social stigma and unproductivity. Under this incentive model, the individual incomes received while unequal would not be unfair. (Marchant et al. 2014, p. 33)

While one can usually come up with many instances regarding how people's actions are motivated by receiving some kind of valued external reward (e.g., working toward a postgraduate degree), it is more difficult to apply that belief to the concept of volunteerism. What motivates the traditional volunteer, however, could be a number of external factors, such as recognition, praise, awards, certificates, and seeing how their work benefits the relevant sector with which the volunteer is involved, a much broader set of value metrics than just money. The key is thus that the external motivator does not have to be money, as long as it has significance and value to the member it benefits. According to economist Stéphanie Lluis, "[i]f well designed, non-monetary rewards do incentivize behavior—sometimes more strongly than money" (Lluis 2015).

A real-life example of putting the idea of an alternative valuation system into play is Zappos. Zappos, the online shoe and apparel company, is testing the waters with a "badge-based compensation" system. Zappos employees will have the opportunity to obtain various kinds of badges, not necessarily tied to higher pay or money. Essentially, the badges give employees the possibility to "expand their roles by earning different badges, giving them both the potential of earning more compensation and pursuing their passions" (Feloni 2015). Employees receive various badges that represent roles and skills they have. Similarly, within the education system, a competitive program was developed a few years ago by a group of foundations to promote the development of digital badges representing a badge-holder's knowledge, skills, accomplishments, and other credentials (Jacobs 2012).

Certainly, the idea of bestowing and receiving a badge in return for an accomplishment is not a novel idea. The Boy and Girl Scouts have been involved in such a practice for years. However, the idea of applying the concept across a society as a way of recognizing valued contributions, by those who are no longer in the labor force, is unique. The badge, which would likely be in digital form, could stand merely for recognition or could be utilized to "purchase" a good, service, or otherwise.

It is likely that some type of social contribution index will eventually need to be created, which classifies and scores individual contributions to society. Badges would be awarded based on each person's social contribution score. To many, such a foreign scheme may seem unnatural and unrealistic. However, it is precisely this and other unorthodox solutions that should be considered, in order to be prepared to address the many complex long-term dimensions of technological unemployment concerns. In fact, a similar system is already in place in China where the government has approved several "social credit" pilot projects that rate an individual's social worthiness. Complex algorithms use online data to amass consumer information and assess a person's likelihood of paying credit card bills, likelihood of success based on the level of education achieved, likelihood of possessing a sense of responsibility based on the types of online purchases that are made, and so forth. The Chinese government expects that by 2020, everyone living in China will be registered in a national "social credit" database (Hatton 2015).

The biggest disadvantage of an alternative valuation method such as granting badges in exchange for social contributions, that in turn may have value as conferring recognition or as a mechanism for exchange, is that it will require creative thinking, at both the implementation level and in terms of public acceptability and adaptability. Whereas today money is globally accepted and valued as a method of exchange, an alternate reward scheme would require a similar agreement and approval. Some might argue that only good can come of ridding ourselves of money, and that the days of big banks, fraud, crime, and corruption would be gone. However, one can imagine that once badges are valued, accepted, and used as a medium of exchange, such problems will not go away. Entities like "badge banks" might come to exist, followed by fraud, crime, and corruption—but likely less so if badges bestowed simply represent recognition of a service or skill. Using the power of big data, analytics, and perhaps even blockchains, badges could be customized and personalized to the earner's needs to prevent some of the problems that are associated with money, such as theft, fraud, and crime.

The function of the badge is another question that would have to be resolved. If it merely represents a token of recognition or achievement, the system that is put in motion would likely be far less complex than if the badge has value as a means of exchange for "upgrades" or non-basic needs. Nonetheless, it remains a potential solution, with details to be worked out, should technology eventually master all or most of upper-, middle-, and low-skill work.

Much remains to be explored, considered, and developed with respect to this Badge proposal. Nevertheless, it or something like it, represents the type of comprehensive, fundamental paradigm shift that will be needed to recognize, reward, and incentivize socially beneficial activities as the central role of the traditional job continues to fade in our era of growing technological sophistication and unemployment.

Conclusion

Now or in the near future, technological unemployment may become a serious problem that, if left unaddressed, threatens to undermine the economic and social foundations of society. Thoughtful and innovative polices will be needed to prevent, mitigate, and overcome this problem. This chapter has identified a series of short-term policy interventions that may be considered, some promising and others less so. But as machines become more powerful and capable, these shorter-term policy solutions will merely be Band-Aids that slow but do not prevent the problem of technological unemployment. To truly address this potential problem, a fundamental change will be needed in the way society values and rewards productive and beneficial activities, and provides for the well-being of its citizens. The "Badge" proposal outlined in the second half of this chapter is intended to start that discussion.

References

ACT Foundation. 2016. *Learning Is Earning*. http://www.learningisearning 2026.org/

Asmundson, Irena, and Ceyda Oner. 2012. What Is Money? *Finance & Development (International Development Fund)* 49(3): 52–53.

Bessen, James. 2015. *Learning by Doing: The Real Connection between Innovation, Wages, and Wealth*. New Haven: Yale University Press.

Dau-Schmidt, Kenneth G. 2001. Employment in the New Age of Trade and Technology: Implications for Labor and Employment Law. *Indiana Law Journal* 76(1): 1–28.

Druckerman, Pamela. 2016. The Miserable French Workplace. *New York Times*, May12.http://www.nytimes.com/2016/05/12/opinion/the-miserable-french-workplace.html?_r=0

Ebdrup, Niels. 2013. We Should Only Work 25 Hours a Week, Argues Professor. *Science Nordic*, February 3. http://sciencenordic.com/we-should-only-work-25-hours-week-argues-professor/

Feloni, Richard. 2015. How Zappos Decides How Much to Pay Employees Under Its New 'Self-Management' System. *Business Insider,* July 24. http://www.businessinsider.com/how-zappos-determines-salaries-in-holacracy-2015-7

Ford, Martin. 2009. *The Lights in the Tunnel: Automation, Accelerating Technology and the Economy of the Future*. Acculant Publishing.

Furchtgott-Roth, Diana. 2015. Generation Y Needs an Office for Inter-Generational Responsibility. *CapX*, July 21. http://capx.co/generation-y-needs-an-office-for-inter-generational-responsibility/

Harris, Seth, and Alan Krueger, 2015. A Proposal for Modernizing Labor Laws for Twenty-First Century Work: The "Independent Worker" The Hamilton Project, Discussion Paper 2015-10. December. http://www.hamiltonproject.org/assets/files/modernizing_labor_laws_for_twenty_first_century_work_krueger_harris.pdf.

Hatton, Celia. 2015. China 'Social Credit': Beijing Sets Up Huge System. *BBC News,* October 26. http://www.bbc.com/news/world-asia-china-34592186

Jacobs, Joanne. 2012. Digital Badges Threaten Colleges' Monopoly on Credentials. *U.S. News & World Report*, January 2.

Kennedy, Joseph V. 2016. Three Paths to Update Labor Law for the Gig Economy. *Information Technology and Innovation Foundation*, April. http://www2.itif.org/2016-labor-law-gig-economy.pdf?_ga=1.254822472.1545933074.1463966997

Ledford, Gerry. 2013. Memo to Dan Pink and Friends: Incentives Do Not Undermine Employee Motivation. *Compensation Café*, May 3. http://www.compensationcafe.com/2013/05/memo-to-dan-pink-and-friends-incentives-do-not-undermine-employee-motivation.html

Lluis, Stéphanie. 2015. Non-Monetary Rewards Cannot Substitute Pay Raises. *Globe & Mail*, August 12.

Marchant, Gary E., Yvonne A. Stevens, and James M. Hennessy. 2014. Technology, Unemployment & Policy Options: Navigating the Transition to a Better World. *Journal of Evolution and Technology* 24(1): 26–44.

P2P Foundation. 2015. *Intrinsic vs. External Motivation*. http://p2pfoundation.net/Intrinsic_vs._Extrinsic_Motivation

Pink, Dan. 2009. The Puzzle of Motivation. *TEDGlobal 2009*, July. http://www.ted.com/talks/dan_pink_on_motivation

Sullivan, S.P. 2014. Timeline: A Brief History of Why You Can't Pump Your Own Gas in New Jersey. *NJ.com*, February 22. http://www.nj.com/news/index. ssf/2014/02/a_brief_history_of_why_you_cant_pump_your_own_gas_in_ new_jersey.html

Tabuchi, Hiroko. 2013. Layoffs Taboo, Japan Workers Are Sent to the Boredom Room. *New York Times*, August 16.

The Venus Project. 2016. *Existing Resources*. https://www.thevenusproject.com/ resource-based-economy/technology/

Tracy, Abigail. 2013. The '40 Hours a Week or Less' Theory Gains Momentum. *Inc. Magazine*, October 10. http://www.inc.com/abigail-tracy/why-you-should-work-less-and-unplug-more.html

U.S. White House. 2011. *Memorandum on Regulatory Flexibility, Small Business, and Job Creation*. January 18. https://www.whitehouse.gov/the-press-office/2011/01/18/presidential-memoranda-regulatory-flexibility-small-business-and-job-cre

Vardi, Moshie Y. 2012. The Consequences of Machine Intelligence. *The Atlantic Online*, October 25. http://www.theatlantic.com/technology/archive/2012/10/ the-consequences-of-machine-intelligence/264066/

Wray, L. Randall. 2011. The Job Guarantee: A Government Plan for Full Employment. *Nation Online*, June 27. http://www.thenation.com/article/ job-guarantee-government-plan-full-employment/

CHAPTER 9

What Is the Job Creation Potential of New Technologies?

James J. Hughes

Until recently, both the beliefs that all human wage labor would be replaced by machines and that we could all live better without wages were very rare. Now these convictions are increasingly held by the technorati, and expressed in the press and popular books such as *Race Against the Machines* by Brynjolfsson and McAfee (2011) *Rise of the Robots* by Martin Ford (2015). Two-thirds of Americans already believe that within the next 50 years computers and robots will displace many of the jobs now done by humans, even if eight in ten Americans still believe their own jobs will be unchanged (Smith 2016). While economists and the policy establishment, from Left to Right, still dismiss the prospect of a jobless future (Furman 2016)—and a consequent need for a basic income guarantee—they are now at least taking the time to officially denigrate those ideas (Council of Economic Advisors 2016).

One of the pieces of research that broke open the debate over automation and employment was the 2013 paper by Carl Benedikt Frey and Michael Osborne, then based at Oxford University. Frey and Osborne dissected 702 American occupations into their component skills, and estimated the likelihood that those skills would be automated in the next two decades (Frey and Osborne 2013). If the bulk of an occupation's skills were automatable it was vulnerable, and they determined that 47% of American jobs were

J.J. Hughes (✉)
University of Massachusetts Boston, Boston, MA, USA
e-mail: jamesj.hughes@umb.edu

© The Author(s) 2017
K. LaGrandeur, J.J. Hughes (eds.), *Surviving the Machine Age*,
DOI 10.1007/978-3-319-51165-8_9

vulnerable to automation. The same methodology has now been applied to European economies (Sproul et al. 2015; Bowles 2014; Frey and Osborne 2014, 2015) and Japan (Jozuka 2015), and finds that roughly a third to half of all jobs in industrialized countries are vulnerable to automation.

Occupations also can harness the power of machines to extend and complement their work, rather than be displaced, to be complemented rather than substituted, or to race *on* the machine rather than *with it*. This is what I want to discuss in this chapter. If the complementarity is successfully managed, the occupation is able to re-focus from the routine tasks to the non-routine tasks, extend the amount of work done by each worker, and reduce the cost of the work. If the work becomes cheap enough, the demand for that occupation may hold steady or increase. An example given for this kind of complementarity is that instead of bank clerks being displaced by ATMs, banks have re-focused on expanding sales and customer service, without any loss in bank clerk numbers.

Jobs That Will Disappear

In the Frey and Osborne analysis, the jobs most at risk are those that involve mostly routine tasks:

- Transport and logistics workers, such as taxi and delivery drivers, at risk from self-driving cars and trucks
- Office support workers, such as receptionists, secretaries, and security guards, at risk from the availability of software substitutes such as automated answering and security systems
- Sales and services workers, such as cashiers, counter and rental clerks, insurance underwriters and appraisers, telemarketers and accountants, also at risk from being replaced by software

On the other hand, the jobs least vulnerable to automation are those that required non-routine manual and cognitive skills that are, as yet, difficult to automate:

- Perceptual judgment and manual dexterity jobs, such as nurses, dentists, and surgeons, as well as cooks and housekeepers
- Social-emotional intelligence jobs, such teachers, managers, therapists, and social workers
- Creative jobs, such as scientists, designers, and people in the visual and performing arts

Subsequent research has shown that the "routineness" of jobs is a good explanation for the growing inequality of wages and uneven employment prospects in the industrialized world. While most economists reject the idea that there is, as yet, any evidence of net job loss, many agree that technological innovation has contributed to growing inequality by disproportionately automating middle-income occupations, driving down both employment in these jobs and their wages, while increasing demand for both non-routine manual labor, and for non-routine cognitive labor that requires higher education and commands high wages (Autor and Dorn 2013; Autor et al. 2003; Goos and Manning 2007; Goos et al. 2014). This is known as the theory of "routinization-biased technological change" (Autor et al. 2003).

For instance, a recent analysis by an economist at the Federal Reserve Bank of St. Louis shows that the number of non-routine cognitive and manual jobs has grown over the past 30 years in the United States, while routine cognitive and manual jobs have not (Dvorkin 2016). In a similar analysis, Levy and Murnane (2013) found that, since 1960, there has been a decline in the proportion of jobs involving Routine Manual Tasks, Routine Cognitive Tasks, and Non-Routine Manual Tasks, but an increase in jobs requiring "Working with New Information" and "Solving Unstructured Problems."

This general pattern has also been found across Europe (Goos et al. 2014), and in studies of specific industries. Looking specifically at the impacts of the implementation of industrial robots in 17 countries and 14 industries between 1993 and 2007, Graetz and Michaels found that robotization reduced the wages and total hours worked by low- and middle-wage workers (Graetz and Michaels 2015). On the other hand, roboticization increased overall production, and expanded employment and wages for more skilled workers, so that there was no net impact on employment.

RACING AGAINST THE MACHINE VERSUS RACING ON THE MACHINE

A critique of the Frey and Osborne analysis has been that just because some of the tasks of a job are automatable does not mean that that job will disappear. Occupations are constantly adapting to new technologies, as the occupants of the occupation turn over the routine tasks to machines, and upskill their work to do more management of machines, and more of their non-routine social, interpersonal, and creative tasks. There is also a division of labor within occupations, such that some jobs within the occupation focus more on the routine work, some more on the non-routine creative work.

One recent analysis that focused on this task/job-based approach was done by economists at the OECD (Arntz et al. 2016), who looked at the automatability of specific jobs within occupations, rather than at the vulnerability of the occupation as a whole. For instance, while the core task of accounting is highly automatable, most accountants regularly interact with clients. If accounting were automated, the OECD team reasoned, the accountants with client contact could spend more time on that, while only those without client contact would be vulnerable to redundancy. Using this approach, the OECD team estimated that only 9% of the jobs in the 21 Organization for Economic Cooperation and Development (OECD) countries were vulnerable to automation, rather than Frey and Osborne's estimate of half of all jobs. A similar analysis by McKinsey (Chui et al. 2015) estimates that while 45% of all current work tasks could be automated, and 60% of occupations could have 30% or more of their constituent activities automated, only 5% of occupations could be entirely automated using current technology.

One way of tracking the adaptation of occupations to technology is when they create new job titles within the occupation. Acemoglu and Restrepo (2016) looked at the creation of new job titles, and found that since 1980 employment growth has been greater in occupations with more new job titles. About half of the growth in employment from 1980 to 2007 came from occupations with new job titles.

Are Professions Safe if They Race *on* the Machine?

Some occupations, such as the professions, have more power to negotiate complementarity with machines than others. Doctors can insist that only they can accurately interpret the work of diagnostic expert systems, or provide telemedicine, so that these technologies extend and complement their work. Secretaries, on the other hand, have far less authority to insist that their bosses can't use answering machines to take calls, or use Doodle to schedule meetings or Expedia to book their travel.

The professions are still potentially vulnerable, however, even if they do insist that technology complement rather than substitute for their work. First, if one doctor or lawyer can use technology to do the work of a dozen, then some doctors and lawyers will be put out of work (Davenport 2015; Davenport and Kirby 2015), unless there are falling prices and rising demand for doctors and lawyers, which poses other problems. Second, if new technologies facilitate competition for providing the service with a national or international market of professionals, then the market will drive down the cost of the service. For instance, 30 million subscribers now use Rocket Lawyer which, for a monthly fee, provides online access to legal advice from a national pool of attorneys, as well as to pre-prepared documents and tutorials. Similarly, telemedicine reduces demand for local specialists by providing access to specialists in cities.

Third, if the professions' work shifts, it undermines the claim that only that profession can do that job. As Susskind and Susskind (2016) argue, a large part of what professions learn in their long educations can be automated. If they increasingly turn those tasks over to machines and focus on the interpersonal aspects of their jobs, or the management of machines, they are vulnerable to competition from less expensive paraprofessionals whose training is as good or better at those interpersonal and machine management tasks. Why pay a doctor for a diagnosis, when a nurse with a computer can provide as good a diagnosis, with twice the patient contact time, and at half the cost?

A survey of 320 law firms in 2015 found widespread optimism about the ability to replace paralegals and junior associates with software (Clay and Seeger 2015). E-discovery methods in law offices allow software to do work in seconds that would have previously taken of dozens of lawyers, clerks, and paralegals months to do (Markoff 2011). The decline in cost for e-discovery has increased the demand for it, so there has been a negligible impact on the number of law clerks. But lawyers, on the other hand, are having a very hard time of it. Remus and Levy (2015) estimate that if just the current artificial intelligence capabilities in law offices were fully implemented, it would reduce legal employment by 13 % (Remus and Levy 2015).

THE KINDS OF JOBS THAT WILL BE ENABLED BY EMERGING TECHNOLOGY

If there is work immune to automation in the future, then, the way to prepare for it is not to focus on the *occupations* that are immune, since the work composition of occupations may change radically, new occupations may emerge, and even the professions are vulnerable to these trends. The proper question is what *skills* will probably still be in demand in the future, as these skills grow in importance within each occupation, or as the core of new occupations.

MacCrory et al. (2014) studied the changes in the skill composition of 674 occupations in the USA between 2006 and 2014. They used a model of seven basic skills: (1) manual dexterity skills, (2) equipment management skills, (3) supervisory skills, (4) visual and perceptual skills, (5) interpersonal skills, (6) "initiative," such as innovation and persistence, and (7) vehicle operation. They found that, through this lens, there has been a decline in demand for perceptual and supervisory skills, and a growth in demand for interpersonal skills and the "equipment" skills required to manage machines. The growing demand for interpersonal skills fits the Frey and Osborne prediction. But the observed decline in demand for perceptual and supervisory skills, and growing demand for machine management skills, were not predicted by the Frey and Osborne model.

Why the Declining Importance of Perceptual Skills in the Technologized Job Market?

One explanation for the declining demand for perceptual skills, which Frey and Osborne assumed were more immune to automation, could be the growing power and application of "deep learning" algorithms, capable of quickly improving their discrimination of the different kinds of people, widgets, or strawberries, and then dealing with them quickly and tirelessly.

Why the Declining Importance of Supervisory Skills?

Likewise, while one might assume that supervising other human beings requires social-emotional intelligence and interpersonal skills, the need to supervise others is quickly being displaced by technology that removes intermediary humans between managers and work. This contradicts the projections of analysts like Frey and Osborne, or the McKinsey group (Chui et al. 2016), that managerial jobs are the least automatable. While jobs requiring "people skills" grew in numbers and earning into the 1990s, demand for those skills slowed in the past two decades (Borghans et al. 2014). Electronic scheduling, communication, and collaboration make it easier to do many things without having a meeting, organizing a team, delegating work, or monitoring subordinates. It is now often easier to tell a machine to do something than to tell human beings. The human manager remains in charge, but without the human subordinates.

The Growing Importance of Interpersonal Competence:

Nonetheless, while supervisory skills are less important, non-routine inter-personal competence in teamwork, collaboration, and communication are increasingly important in working directly with clients and co-workers. For instance, Catherine Weinberger (2014) linked tests of adolescents' skills done in 1972 and 1992 to their subsequent career outcomes. She found that both math skills and social skills independently predicted sub-sequent career success and income. But intriguingly, there was a strong interaction effect as well. In other words, adolescents who were strong in *both* math and social skills earned 10% more than their peers who were only strong in one of those two domains. Deming (2015) links the grow-ing importance of social skills to the technology-driven rise of flexible and self-managed teams, job rotation, and worker multitasking. In Deming's model, social skills are both non-routine, and as yet non-automatable, and they reduce the costs associated with building the new lateral models of providing services.

The Growing Importance of Computing and Machine Skills

Bessen (2015) has documented that computer-intensive jobs are grow-ing and displacing more labor-intensive jobs. Occupations that use com-puters are also paid better. Computerization re-allocates work from the occupations not using them to the occupations that are using them, rais-ing the premium on computer skills. One example is the ability to organize and present data with statistical and graphical tools. As the management of human beings declines in importance, however, the skills required to manage the work of machines becomes ever more important.

The Growing Importance of Creative and Cognitive Skills

A survey of employers conducted by the World Economic Forum in 2015 found a steep increase in demand for cognitive abilities, systems skills, and complex problem solving skills—such as math and logical reasoning, visu-alization, systems analysis, and creativity—by 2020 (WEF 2016).

In *Creativity* versus *the Robots,* Bakhshi et al. (2015) categorized 120 occupations according to whether they used imagination or original ideas to create something. In their accounting, one in five US jobs is highly creative, including jobs such as architects, artists and web designers, IT specialists, and public relations professionals. (I would take issue with their judgment that "Actuaries, economists and statisticians" and "Social and humanities scientists" are not creative occupations. Writing an essay like this requires some creativity doesn't it?) For the UK, their estimate was that one in four jobs was highly creative. Using their model of computerization risk, they estimate that almost all of these highly creative jobs (86%) were at no or low risk of automation.

POTENTIAL NEW JOBS CREATED BY TECHNOLOGY, AND SOME POTENTIAL HICCUPS

So if there are some areas of human social, cognitive, and creative skills that are immune to automation for the time being, what kinds of jobs might appear that would utilize those skills? By definition, it is hard to imagine jobs that don't exist yet, but there have been some comedic attempts to imagine such jobs. One effort, written by Stanley Bing, was published in the July 2016 *Fortune* magazine and titled "Hot Jobs for 2020 and Beyond." His list, albeit satiric, illustrates the problem of imagining truly novel occupations:

- "Identity brokers" to massage your social media persona, and "online shaming consultants" to help orchestrate online shaming campaigns. Both are really just extensions of existing public relations and political consulting jobs, applied to social media, and perhaps made more widely accessible by being gig-ified.
- "Brain rebooters" would be experts at rehabilitating brains damaged by cognitive enhancement, although it's hard to see why existing neurology and psychiatry wouldn't capture this market.
- "Funeral directors on Mars" would likewise just be an existing occupation transplanted.

On a more serious note, the Australian government published a report on "Tomorrow's Digitally Enabled Workforce" in January 2016 (Hajkowic et al. 2016; Myers 2016). Their proposals for new or expanding occupations are:

- Data analysts and customer experience experts: This is welcome news for a quantitative social scientist like myself, although the current thrust of business intelligence software is precisely to simplify the collection of unstructured consumer data, reducing dependence on survey and focus group researchers, and to eliminate the need for analysts by putting data visualization tools directly in decision-makers' hands (Baker 2016).

- Remote-controlled vehicle operators: These would be pilots, captains, and drivers who would remotely monitor self-driving planes, ships, and trucks. This is more of a re-tasking of a minority of lucky existing workers, rather than a new occupation.
- Personalized preventative health helpers, to help people navigate and apply health information and technologies: This is a role already occupied by nurses, dieticians, physical therapists, and personal trainers, although there might be a niche for a technology-focused hybrid of these occupations, for those who can afford it.
- Online chaperones to protect individuals from identity theft and to manage online reputations, similar to Bing's satiric "identity brokers." Since anti-virus and Malware software do the cybersecurity part of the job automatically and far more effectively, and there are already firms offering online identity management, this seems like an unlikely growth industry.

If we are unable to imagine truly novel occupations, perhaps we can think about future jobs in terms of economic sectors. As paid private sector employment declines, there will be a growing demand for part-time, on-demand work and public sector employment.

Gig Economy Jobs

In the emerging gig economy enabled by Internet disintermediation, all jobs will be less secure and an ever-greater portion of the workforce will become part-time, on-demand, independent contractors without benefits (Hill 2015). According to research by Katz and Krueger (2016), the growth of gig employment outpaced the growth of full-time US employment between 2005 and 2015. Even if there is no net decline in "employment," if these trends continue, they portend an increasing polarization between more secure highly paid jobs and less secure, part-time, low-wage jobs. Some gig-ified occupations that we can expect to grow are:

- Transportation, as Uber drivers displace cab drivers.
- Accommodation, as services such as Airbnb replace full-time hotel work.

- Manufacturing, as part-time shift workers replace full-time employees.
- Research, as "mechanical Turk" pieceworkers replace full-time research jobs.
- Human Services, as on-demand house cleaners and home aides replace workers with full-time contracts.

Public Sector Jobs

Benzell et al. (2015) have modeled that increasing productivity from automation (Sirkin et al. 2015) with a consequent decline of employment will produce a classic "crisis of overproduction," with impoverished consumers unable to keep the economy growing. Demands are already growing for the redistribution of wealth through a universal basic income, and these demands will likely grow as technological unemployment becomes more apparent. But most countries will likely first attempt Keynesian stimulus through expanding public employment.

Currently, a vigorous expansion of public employment seems politically unrealistic. But governments are likely to respond to technological unemployment with attempts to expand public employment and national service for the young. Clearly, there are many social and infrastructural needs that could be addressed with corps of road-builders, tree-planters, and care-givers for the elderly people.

A Caveat: The Possible Decline of Public Sector Employment

If public sector jobs are more cheaply and ably fulfilled by road-building and tree-planting robots, or telemedicine for seniors, then calls for more public employment may be politically indefensible. The increasing efficiency of computerized public sector work may already be an explanation for its decline. The number of USA postal workers has, for instance, more than halved in the past decade. Although the number of non-military workers in the US federal government, including postal workers, is the same, two and a half million, than it was in the 1960s, today that is only 2% of the population compared to 4.3% in 1966. Including state and local employees, the proportion of public employees in the population has fallen from 10% in 2000 to a 30-year low of 9%. Likewise, public sector employment has fallen throughout the industrialized world in response to post-2008 austerity measures.

Another way that governments used to absorb the army of the unemployed was military service. But the size of militaries in the industrialized world has also declined as militaries shifted to more capital-intensive military infrastructure. Since the 1950s, the US military has shrunk by half, from 3 million active duty military personnel to 1.4 million today. The EU has seen a reduction of military personnel from 2.5 million in 1999 to 2 million today. The growing use of military drones and robotics also reduces the need for infantry, and the US Army projects that military robotics will displace a quarter of combat soldiers by 2030 (Atherton 2014).

Elder Care

Demographic changes and longevity therapies will increase the proportion of the population needing geriatric services and assistance with daily living, while pensions and private long-term care insurance policies will not be able to fund these needed services. So publicly financed geriatric care will be a likely way to absorb discouraged workers. Many of the physical and cognitive skills involved in nursing and social services for seniors are too complex to be amenable to automation (Chui et al. 2016), although some, like collecting patient information, are automatable. Since home health aides and nursing assistants only make about $20,000–$25,000 per year, it will take a while before robots are cheap enough to offset their wages.

Infrastructure Work

There are a raft of studies demonstrating that there are enormous unmet needs for maintaining and replacing the public infrastructure of the USA, from roads and bridges to waste-management and high-speed rail. Europe spends twice as much of their GDP on infrastructure, and China spends four times as much (Woetzel et al. 2016). In their 2013 Infrastructure Report Card, the American Society for Civil Engineers (ASCE 2013) advised that the USA needs to invest some $3.6 trillion by 2020 to upgrade our infrastructure.

FINAL THOUGHTS

Predicting how automation and myriad other emerging technologies may expand employment can only be done in broad strokes, and I'm not very optimistic that in the long run any of the new occupations will provide as much employment as the jobs that technology displaces. But insofar as there will be as yet unimagined occupations, we can safely predict that they will rely on the skills least vulnerable to automation, namely, higher-order human cognition and creativity, and jobs involved in making, maintaining, and managing new technologies. The lifelong career will continue to decline as the part-time, Internet-enabled gig economy grows. There will also be pressure to expand employment in the public sector, at least in occupations relatively immune to automation, such as care for the elderly population. The extent to which we prepare the next generation for this rapidly evolving labor market will determine how much economic pain we can avoid in the coming decades.

REFERENCES

Acemoglu, Daron, and Pascual Restrepo. 2016. The Race Between Man and Machine: Implications of Technology for Growth, Factor Shares and Employment. MIT, October 2015. https://bfi.uchicago.edu/sites/default/files/research/Man_Vs_Machine_October_16_2015.pdf

Arntz, Melanie, Terry Gregory, and Ulrich Zeirahn. 2016. The Risk of Automation for Jobs in OECD Countries: A Comparative Analysis. OECD Social, Employment and Migration Working Papers, No. 189. Paris: OECD Publishing. doi:10.1787/5jlz9h56dvq7

ASCE. 2013. Report Card for America's Infrastructure. ASCE. http://www.infrastructurereportcard.org/executive-summary/

Atherton, Kelsey D. 2014. Robots May Replace One-Fourth of U.S. Combat Soldiers By 2030, Says General. *Popular Science*, January 1. http://www.popsci.com/article/technology/robots-may-replace-one-fourth-us-combat-soldiers-2030-says-general

Autor, David H., and David Dorn. 2013. The Growth of Low Skill Service Jobs and the Polarisation of the U.S. Labor Market. *American Economic Review* 103(5): 1553–1597.

Autor, David H., Frank Levy, and Richard J. Murnane. 2003. The Skill Content of Recent Technological Change: An Empirical Exploration. *Quarterly Journal of Economics* 118(4): 1279–1333.

Baker, Anthony. 2016. What Does Artificial Intelligence Mean for the Creative Mind? *The Guardian*, August 10. https://www.theguardian.com/medianetwork/2016/aug/10/artificialintelligencethenewcreativemind

Bakhshi, Hasan, Carl B. Frey, and Michael Osborne. 2015. *Creativity vs. Robots*. Nesta. http://www.nesta.org.uk/sites/default/files/creativity_vs._robots_wv.pdf

Benzell, Seth G., Laurence J. Kotliko, Guillermo LaGarda, and Jeffrey D. Sachs. 2015. Robots Are Us: Some Economics of Human Replacement. NBER Working Paper No. 20941. March 29, 2015. http://www.nber.org/papers/w20941

Bessen, James. 2015. How Computer Automation Affects Occupations: Technology, Jobs and Skills. Law & Economics Working Paper No. 15–49, Boston University School of Law.

Borghans, Lex, Bas Ter Weel, and Bruce A. Weinberg, 2014. People skills and the labor-market outcomes of underrepresented groups. *Industrial & Labor Relations Review* 67(2): 287–334.

Bowles, Jeremy. 2014. The Computerisation of European Jobs. *Bruegel*, July 24, 2014. http://www.bruegel.org/nc/blog/detail/article/1394-the-computerisation-of-european-jobs

Brynjolfsson, Erik, and Andrew McAfee. 2011. *Race Against the Machine*. Digital Frontier Press. Kindle edition.

Chui, Michael, James Manyika, and Mehdi Miremadi. 2015. Four Fundamentals of Workplace Automation, McKinsey and Company. http://www.mckinsey.com/business-functions/business-technology/our-insights/four-fundamentals-of-workplace-automation

———. 2016. Where Machines Could Replace Humans—And Where They Can't (Yet), McKinsey and Company. http://www.mckinsey.com/business-functions/business-technology/our-insights/

Clay, Thomas, and Eric Seeger. 2015. 2015 Law Firms in Transition. Altman Weil. http://www.altmanweil.com/dir_docs/resource/1c789ef2-5cff-463a-863a-2248d23882a7_document.pdf

Council of Economic Advisors. 2016. *Economic Report of the President*. Washington, DC. https://www.whitehouse.gov/sites/default/files/docs/ERP_2016_Book_Complete%20JA.pdf

Davenport, Thomas. 2015. Let's Automate All the Lawyers? *Wall Street Journal*, March 25. http://blogs.wsj.com/cio/2015/03/25/lets-automate-all-the-lawyers/

Davenport, Thomas H., and Julia Kirby. 2015. Beyond Automation. *Harvard Business Review*, June. https://hbr.org/2015/06/beyond-automation

Deming, David J. 2015. The Growing Importance of Social Skills in the Labor Market. NBER Working Paper No. 21473, National Bureau of Economic Research, August. http://www.nber.org/papers/w21473

Dvorkin, Maximiliano. 2016. Jobs Involving Routine Tasks Aren't Growing. St. Louis: Federal Reserve Bank of St. Louis, January 4. https://www.stlouisfed.org/on-the-economy/2016/january/jobs-involving-routine-tasks-arent-growing

Ford, Martin. 2015. *Rise of the Robots: Technology and the Threat of a Jobless Future*. New York: Basic Books.

Frey, Carl Benedikt, and Michael A. Osborne. 2013. *The Future of Employment: How Susceptible Are Jobs to Computerisation?* Oxford: Oxford Martin School Working Paper.

———. 2014. Agiletown: The Relentless March of Technology and London's Response. *London Futures*. Deloitte, November. http://www2.deloitte.com/

uk/en/pages/growth/articles/agiletown-the-relentless-march-of-technology-and-londons-response.html#
———. 2015. Technology at Work: The Future of Innovation and Employment, Oxford Martin School.
Furman, Jason. 2016. Is This Time Different? The Opportunities and Challenges of Artificial Intelligence, Remarks at AI Now: The Social and Economic Implications of Artificial Intelligence Technologies in the Near Term, New York University, New York, July 7.
Goos, Maarten, and Alan Manning. 2007. Lousy and Lovely Jobs: The Rising Polarization of Work in Britain. *Review of Economics and Statistics* 89: 118–133.
Goos, Maarten, Alan Manning, and Anna Salomons. 2014. Explaining Job Polarization: Routine-Biased Technological Change and Offshoring. *American Economic Review* 104(8): 2509–2526.
Graetz, George, and Guy Michaels. 2015. Robots at Work. Center for Economic Performance. CEP Discussion Paper No. 1335, March. http://cep.lse.ac.uk/pubs/download/dp1335.pdf
Hajkowic, Stefan, Andrew Reeson, Lachlan Rudd, Alexandra Bratanova, Leonie Hodgers, Claire Mason, and Naomi Boughen. 2016. Tomorrow's Digitally Enabled Workforce: Megatrends and Scenarios for Jobs and Employment in Australia Over the Coming Twenty Years. *Australian Policy Online*, CSIRO, Brisbane, February 4. http://apo.org.au/resource/tomorrows-digitally-enabled-workforce-megatrends-and-scenarios-jobs-and-employment
Hill, Steven. 2015. The Future of Work in the Uber Economy: Creating a Safety Net in a Multi-Employer World, *Boston Review*, July 22, 2015. https://bostonreview.net/us/steven-hill-uber-economy-individual-security-accounts
Jozuka, Emiko. 2015. Robots Could Take Over Nearly 50 Percent of Jobs in Japan in the Next 20 Years. *Motherboard*, December 3.
Katz, Lawrence, and Alan Krueger. 2016. The Rise and Nature of Alternative Work Arrangements in the United States, 1995–2015. Princeton University and NBER.
Levy, Frank, and Richard Murnane. 2013. Dancing with Robots: Human Skills for Computerized Work. *Third Way*. http://www.thirdway.org/report/dancing-with-robots-human-skills-for-computerized-work
MacCrory, Frank, George Westerman, Yousef Alhammadi, and Eric Brynjolfsson. 2014. Racing with and Against the Machine: Changes in Occupational Skill Composition in an Era of Rapid Technological Advance. Thirty Fifth International Conference on Information Systems, Auckland.
Markoff, John. 2011. Armies of Expensive Lawyers, Replaced by Cheaper Software. *New York Times*, March 4. http://www.nytimes.com/2011/03/05/science/05legal.html
Myers, Joe. 2016. What New Jobs Will Exist in 2035? *World Economic Forum*, February. https://www.weforum.org/agenda/2016/02/these-scientists-have-predicted-which-jobs-will-be-human-only-in-2035/

Remus, Dana, and Frank Levy. 2015. Can Robots Be Lawyers? Computers, Lawyers, and the Practice of Law. *Social Science Research Network*, December 30. http://ssrn.com/abstract=2701092

Sirkin, Harold L., Michael Zinser, and Justin Rose. 2015. Why Advanced Manufacturing Will Boost Productivity. Boston Consulting Group, January 30. https://www.bcgperspectives.com/content/articles/lean_and_manufacturing_production_ why_advanced_manufacturing_boost_productivity/

Smith, Aaron. 2016. Public Predictions for the Future of Workforce Automation. *Pew Research Center.* http://www.pewinternet.org/2016/03/10/public-predictions-for-the-future-of-workforce-automation/

Sproul, David, Angus Knowles-Cutler, Harvey Lewis. 2015. From Brawn to Brains: The Impact of Technology on Jobs in the UK. *Deloitte.* http://www2.deloitte.com/uk/en/pages/growth/articles/from-brawn-to-brains--the-impact-of-technology-on-jobs-in-the-u.html

Susskind, Richard, and Daniel Susskind. 2016. *The Future of the Professions: How Technology Will Transform the Work of Human Experts.* Oxford: Oxford University Press.

Weinberger, Catherine J. 2014. The Increasing Complementarity Between Cognitive and Social Skills. *The Review of Economics and Statistics* 96(5): 849–861. doi:10.1162/REST_a_00449.

Woetzel, Jonathan, Nicklas Garemo, Jan Mischke, Martin Hjerpe, and Robert Palter. 2016. Bridging Global Infrastructure Gaps. McKinsey Global Institute. McKinsey and Company, June. http://www.mckinsey.com/industries/capital-projects-and-infrastructure/our-insights/bridging-global-infrastructure-gaps

World Economic Forum. 2016. The Future of Jobs: Employment, Skills and Workforce Strategy for the Fourth Industrial Revolution. Global Challenge Insight Report. *World Economic Forum.* http://www3.weforum.org/docs/WEF_Future_of_Jobs.pdf

Rage Against the Machine: Rethinking Education in the Face of Technological Unemployment

David J. Gunkel

Analysts debate the impact that emerging technology will have on the future of jobs. One side argues that the transformations wrought by this next wave of automation or technological unemployment will follow the historic precedent of previous economic upheavals since the advent of industrialization—temporary job loss followed by overall gains in new opportunities. The other side asserts that things will be different this time around and that we will need to be prepared for what Martin Ford (2015) has called a "jobless future." No matter the exact outcome (which will probably reside somewhere in between these two extreme alternatives), it will certainly have an effect on education and the task of preparing and credentialing individuals for employment. In fact, a recently published Pew Research Center report found considerable disagreement among experts concerning the impact of automation on future employment opportunity. But the one thing all respondents agreed on was the immediate and pressing need to rethink education: "Our public institutions—especially our educational system—are not adequately prepared for the coming wave of technological change" (Pew Research Center 2014, 55).

D.J. Gunkel (✉)
Department of Communication, Northern Illinois University, Chicago, IL, USA
e-mail: dgunkel@niu.edu

　　　　　　　　　　　　　　　　　　　　147
K. LaGrandeur, J.J. Hughes (eds.), *Surviving the Machine Age*,
DOI 10.1007/978-3-319-51165-8_10

The following chapter argues for a recalibration of education to meet the demands of the twenty-first century by (1) identifying two major challenges to existing concepts, structures, and methodologies and (2) describing updates and modifications ("mods") that can be instituted to respond to these opportunities. The use of the terms "update" and "mod" in this context might need some clarification. In computer software, especially games, "updates" are official changes to a program's underlying structure. They are "top-down" reformulations or patches developed and implemented by the institution in order to retool or rework the system's basic operations. "Mods," by contrast, are end-user modifications that are designed to make a program function in ways not conceived of or intended by the original manufacturer. In other words, mods are bottom-up (and often unauthorized) hacks aimed at repurposing the existing system to better respond to and facilitate the actual needs of users. Following this precedent, this chapter will consider both updates and mods for existing educational systems. Updates are necessary insofar as there are important structural changes that can only be made at the institutional level. These changes, however, often take considerable time and effort to develop and implement successfully. Mods are necessary to respond to this problem. The opportunities and challenges of emerging technology are far too important, influential, and rapid for students and teachers to have the luxury to wait for top-down institutional changes. For this reason, mods are deployed to rework the existing system in order to make it respond to and serve more immediate concerns.[1]

GAINFULLY UNEMPLOYED

In a widely publicized study from the Oxford Martin School, Carl Benedikt Frey and Michael A. Osborne (2013) predict that 47 % of jobs in the United States are at risk of being automated out of existence. The exact impact of this potentially massive job loss is something that remains open to debate: Will this be a momentary hiatus in employment opportunities, or will this unemployment be the "new normal" with a much larger percentage of the adult population not working? What is not debated, however, is the fact that there could be a significant number of adults who will, at one time or another, be unemployed or underemployed. In response to the economic and social pressures exerted by this, researchers like Wendell Wallach (2015) and Martin Ford (2015) have advocated for alternative forms of capital redistribution. The argument is rather simple and direct. As employment opportunity is increasingly threatened by emerging technology, "the mechanisms that get purchasing power into the hands of consumers begins to break down, and demand for products and services suffer" (Ford 2015, 264). If this breakdown in purchasing power is more than just a temporary setback, it could destabilize the national economies and threaten existing social structures. "If technological unemployment outstrips job creation," Wallach argues, "forward-thinking governments could forestall political unrest through some form of capital redistribution such as a robust welfare system or guaranteed minimum income" (2015, 159). And there are a handful of "universal basic income" pilot projects currently being tested in places like Ontario, Canada (Cowburn 2016), and Holland (Diez 2015).

But throwing money at the problem is not necessarily the solution. Work is not just a matter of wealth redistribution and "purchasing power." It is also connected to and involved with personal identity and social standing. In fact, as it has been formulated in "the protestant work ethic," working is a moral obligation and unemployment is generally perceived to be a personal failure. In the United States, for example, "the unemployed" (already a problematic term) are typically situated in political debates not as individuals displaced by inequities in the current system of employment opportunity but as social parasites looking for a handout from the government. As a result, unemployment, even temporary unemployment, has a less than laudable social profile. But this perception is just that; it is a perception. It is a matter of the way individuals have been educated—formally within school and informally in contemporary culture—to think about work and its social value. It is, in other words, a matter of ideology. The real challenge, then, is to reconfigure education to prepare students not just for employment but also for unemployment, whether long-term or temporary. Although it may sound counter-intuitive, we need to teach individuals and our culture as a whole how to be both employed and gainfully unemployed. And the fact that this idea seems counter-intuitive is sufficient evidence that we do not yet have a clue as to how one goes about doing this or why.

Compare, for instance, the "promise" of widespread unemployment to the reality of being out of work. In a TED talk from 2012, Andrew McAfee, co-author with Erik Brynjolfsson of *The Second Machine Age*, paints a rather utopian picture of technological unemployment: "So, yeah, the droids are taking our jobs, but focusing on that fact misses the point entirely. The point is that then we are freed up to do other things, and what we're going to do, I am very confident, what we're going to do is reduce poverty and drudgery and misery around the world." But what actually happens when individuals are "freed" from the drudgery of work? Currently the vast majority of unemployed men (in the United States, at least) spend the day in their pajamas watching television (Halpern 2015, 6). Emerging technology, therefore, promises to liberate us from the drudgery of work, but we do not necessarily know what can or should be done with all this new "free time."

System Updates

There are at least two institutional changes that will be necessary to respond to this challenge. First, we need to devise broad-based education programs that can address both opportunities for work and the challenges of being without work. Recent initiatives in higher education have given increased emphasis (and funding) to specializations in the STEM (Science Technology Engineering Math) fields, and for good reasons: that is where the best employment opportunities have been situated. In this effort, however, many universities have found it necessary to curtail or significantly modify requirements in the social sciences and humanities. In one of the more visible signs of this development, Japan's minister of education, Hakubun Shimomura, called on his nation's 86 public universities either to discontinue programs in the social sciences and humanities "or to convert them to serve areas that better meet society's needs" (Grove 2015). Though there has been considerable debate about the exact impact this directive will have on the shape of higher education within Japan (Steffensen 2015), it is an indication of the way competing priorities are being addressed at a time of increased budgetary stress. Cultivating specialization in one of the STEM fields is undoubtedly necessary for preparing students to be able to deal with the opportunities and challenges of working with emerging technology. But this should not be done at the expense of other forms of instruction that can help provide the context for understanding and dealing with the social impact and consequences of employing these systems. Education is not and should not be a zero-sum game. As Russell Bailey, the director of the library at Providence College, reported to the Pew Research Center: "The propensity for narrow job-training instead of broader career-training will restrict and limit employability for many, until or unless they accept longer-range, broader career-training as the default path to ongoing employability" (Pew Research Center 2014, p. 55). For this reason, the future may belong to a new kind of broadly educated professional. Not simply because these individuals will, as Arun Sundararajan (2016) argues, be more adequately prepared to take advantage of new forms of self-employment in the "sharing economy" or "crowd based capitalism" (6), but also because it provides individuals with the knowledge and skill to make sense of and work through those periods of time when one might not be working or have access to gainful employment. To put it in McAfee's terms, if individuals liberated from the drudgery of work will be "freed up to do other things," we may need a more active effort to define and develop what "other things" can be done and are worth doing.

Second, we need to re-think the neo-liberal narrative that has, for better or worse, come to shape the way education is currently conceptualized and funded. Typically higher education, especially in the United States, has been marketed and justified in terms of "hire education." Promoted in this fashion, education is routinely situated as a personal investment and, for this reason, students are able, theoretically at least, to justify going into debt to fund the opportunity. But if employment after graduation becomes less certain, it becomes increasingly difficult to justify making expenditures that will have little or even no return on investment. As of 2014, US student-loan debt totaled in excess of $1.1 trillion dollars, which averages out to $30,000 per student (White House 2014; Lorin 2016). In order to maintain this system—and to do so at a time when universities and colleges have increasingly come to rely on student tuition for basic operating revenue—there will need to be a steady stream of high-paying jobs available to graduates, both to ensure repayment of existing loans and to convince future students to participate in the program. In the face of increasing employment uncertainty and instability, however, it is hard to sustain this system, without the entire thing becoming a pyramid scheme. In order to respond to this, we will need, on the one hand, to revise the narrative of higher education, repositioning education as a public good and not a personal investment, and, on the other hand, to devise practical methods for publicly funding education that does not shift the burden to individual students. The former is a task for educators and public policy makers, and it concerns the narratives we tell ourselves about education and its social value. The purpose of public education, within the framework of the USA at least, was always to produce informed citizens capable of carrying out the task of self-governance. And as the challenges of self-governance increase, with the need to sort out and make sense of things like self-driving cars, nanotechnology, and learning algorithms, so too does the responsibility to provide citizens with the necessary knowledge and data to make informed decisions. For these reasons, the proper funding of public education is neither optional nor a luxury for the few, it is one of the fundamental responsibilities of twenty-first-century democratic governments.

User-Generated Mods

Curricular modifications and alternative funding schemes are clearly going to be necessary. But getting traction with these large-scale systemic changes is not going to be easy or quick. In the interim, students and teachers need "boots on the ground" solutions that can be implemented in the short-term, if not immediately. First, and concerning what happens at the classroom level, faculty can and should begin to incorporate critical reflection on employment, personal identity, and social status in their courses. The coupling of identity and work is culturally and historically specific; it is based on particular ideological formations that have a long and rather successful history behind them. Instructors should neither take these arrangements for granted nor perpetuate their influence by remaining silent on the subject. We need to identify and make these assumptions the explicit object of investigation, irrespective of the discipline or field. In other words, individual teachers have the opportunity to get their students actively involved in thinking about work, the significance it has within contemporary culture, and the way that it interacts with our own understanding of identity and social responsibility. This direct engagement with and critique of the ideology of "hire education" is necessary not to undermine the usual way of doing things but to empower students to understand how their expectations have been organized and why. Achieving this objective can be accomplished in the university classroom rather easily by asking students to reflect on and respond to the question "Why am I here?" This inquiry, which can be pursued either as a short writing project or in discussion, is not only a good way to begin a new semester—a kind of "ice-breaking" exercise—but offers students the opportunity to articulate and examine the often unquestioned assumptions about education and its role in their lives.

Second, students also play a crucial role in this "modding" of education. The link between education—higher education in particular—and employment is something that is (again for very understandable reasons) widely recognized by the student population, especially those individuals who are first-generation university students. For several generations now, the official story has been persistent and consistent: better education = better jobs. As the connection between education and employment opportunity begins to unravel or at least loosen up to such an extent that the one is not necessarily and directly related to the other, students and their families will need to re-examine what they believe education is for. Though this effort might seem to be a pressing concern for students pursuing studies in the liberal and fine arts, it is becoming increasingly necessary in many of the professional fields that had been situated as directly feeding into employment opportunity, that is, law and business. According to a report published in May 2016, the law firm BakerHostetler "hired" an implementation of IBM's Watson to assist with research for the firm's bankruptcy cases. The artificial intelligence (AI), affectionately named "Ross," is expected to take the place of a large cohort of human paralegals and attorneys (Turner 2016). Similar displacements are occurring in the financial services industry, where algorithms are now being used not just for the routine work of the office clerk but also for research and analysis and direct client relations (Popper 2016). "We are," explains Daniel Nadler of the financial start-up Kensho, "creating a very small number of high-paying jobs in return for destroying a very large number of fairly high-paying jobs, and the net-net to society, absent some sort of policy intervention or new industry that no one's thought of yet to employ all those people, is a net loss" (Popper 2016). In other words, automation will not displace all employment opportunities; there will continue to be a few very good paying jobs at the high end of the spectrum. But the entry-level and middle-management positions that have traditionally been the target of professional education will be in increasingly short supply.

Challenging prevailing assumptions is no easy task, especially when tuition and fees constitute a significant financial burden. Nevertheless, we need to begin questioning or at least developing some critical perspective on the "education means employment opportunity" narrative. In effect, we need to decide—each one of us individually and together—"What is education for?" Although this might initially look like an existential crisis for institutions of higher education, it is really about the needs and expectations of those individuals and communities that these institutions serve.

DIY FUTURES

At the same time that we begin to question and challenge the assumed tight coupling of education and work, we will also need to recognize that whatever new opportunities develop in the wake of emerging technology, they will certainly require some form of preparation. The problem for educators is that we often find ourselves in the odd position of needing to devise curriculum and pedagogical opportunities for occupations that do not yet exist or at least are not yet fully realized so that one might know what will be needed in terms of skills and knowledge. But this is only a problem if we think about education as responding to the needs of industry as it is currently configured or imagined. There is another way to look at it, which has the effect of reversing the direction of thethis vector.

Consider two rather remarkable examples from the last wave of technological innovation. When Marc Andreessen was a student at the University of Illinois, he did not pursue a major in e-commerce or complete course work necessary to get a job with an Internet company. Neither of these existed. Instead, he, along with Eric Bina (who unfortunately often gets left out of the story), created NSCA Mosaic, the first graphical Web browser, which became one of the enabling technologies of e-commerce and helped make the Internet companies of the 1990s tech-explosion possible in the first place. The same might be said for Facebook CEO, Mark Zuckerberg. Zuckerberg, who attended but did not graduate from Harvard University, did not pursue a degree in social media in hopes of landing a job with one of the major players in the industry. He helped invent social media by hacking together the PHP code that eventually became Facebook. Clearly these examples are the exception and not the rule. But they indicate a different way to think about higher education and its relationship to employment. Instead of preparing individuals to take advantage of existing opportunities—opportunities that are volatile insofar as they might not exist by the time current students matriculate—we need to develop educational structures that also encourage and help students to invent the future.

System Updates

Getting students actively involved in innovation is nothing new. This has been and remains one of the principal objectives and the *raison d'etre* of the research university. But institutions can and should be doing much more to encourage and support this kind of entrepreneurial activity, especially when it comes to technology transfer and commercialization policies. Although universities have long been involved in commercializing innovations developed by their faculty and students, it has only been since the 1970s that policies and offices dedicated to this effort have been institutionalized. This development received significant legislative support when, in 1980, the US Congress passes the Bayh-Dole Act, which shifted ownership of Federally funded research (i.e. NSF, NEH, NIH) from the US government to the university where the research project was conducted.

University ownership has distinct advantages for both the researcher and the institution. For the researcher, whether she/he is a member of the faculty or a student using university facilities and resources, the technology licensing office (TLO), as these facilities are commonly called, provides assistance in obtaining the necessary IP (intellectual property) protections and arranging licensing agreements with third parties. In effect, the TLO provides a technology transfer and commercialization service. For the institution, the TLO has become an important revenue-generating resource. One of the most widely studied and lucrative university-owned patents is the Cohen-Boyer (C-B) patent, which involves techniques for the creation of genetically engineered microorganisms. "Over its 17-year life," Martin Kenny and Donald Patton (2009, 1409) write, "C-B produced in excess of $255 million in revenues for Stanford University and the University of California."

Despite (or perhaps because of) this success, recent studies of existing models and commercialization policies find numerous contradictions, inconsistencies, and misaligned incentives. As Kenney and Patton (2009, 1413) explain: "The licensing experience of Marc Andreessen....illustrates the pitfalls. When Andreessen joined James Clark to form Netscape in 1994, they attempted to negotiate a license with the University of Illinois but found the process so frustrating that they ultimately rewrote the browser code entirely." Meanwhile, successfully negotiated licensing agreements with other corporations, like Microsoft, who used the original Mosaic code as part of their Internet Explorer browser, netted the University of Illinois a total of $7 million. If students have difficulties using, developing, or licensing the innovations they have developed or have helped develop, then the existing commercialization policies cease being a useful service and start interfering with future opportunities.

For this reason, universities need either to reform the current system or to devise alternative models for research commercialization. Kenny and

Patton (2009), for their part, suggest two alternatives: vesting ownership with the individual inventor or placing all university-produced innovation in the public domain and available, without restriction, to any and all users. The former "would remove research commercialization from the control and mission of the university administration and would decentralize it to the inventors" (1415). Under the latter, "the university administration would no longer be involved in licensing, [and] the university would return to its role as a platform for research and instruction" (1414). Although neither model necessarily does away with the university TLO, they do introduce a significant shift in who owns and controls the products of university research and innovation. Consequently there are good reasons to believe that universities might not be entirely satisfied with these particular alternatives. "While meant to be used for further research," Kenny and Patton explain, "TLO income is attractive to administrators because the funds are, in fact, largely unencumbered, thereby providing wide discretion on how they are spent. Often the support monies for TLO personnel can originate from public funds, either federal or state. This asymmetry offers a powerful incentive—restricted funds can be spent to operate the TLO, while earnings are far less restricted. The strength of this incentive is difficult to measure, but it may be considerable as more flexible funds are invariably in short supply" (2009, 1410). What is needed, therefore, is to formulate some reasonable balance between the financial interests of the institution and the rights of faculty and students to develop and commercialize their own innovations.

User-Generated Mods

As with the first set of updates, this restructuring of the policies and procedures of innovation ownership and commercialization is not going to be resolved quickly or effortlessly. For this reason, students and teachers also need more immediate bottom-up strategies. First and foremost, students should know and understand their university's policy for technology transfer and commercialization. Although most, if not all, institutions of higher education have some explicit policy regarding this, not all universities are created equal. In most cases, employees of the university (i.e. faculty, graduate assistants, research assistants) are required, as part of their employment contract, to disclose and assign ownership of their efforts to the university. The same requirement does not necessarily apply to students. This does not mean, however, that student innovation is automatically exempt. At many institutions, student research is exempt only in cases where the innovation was produced without the use of *significant* university resources or facilities. MIT (2016), for instance, provides the following stipulation: "When an invention, software, or other copyrightable material, mask work, or tangible research property is developed by M.I.T. faculty, students, staff, visitors or others participating in M.I.T. programs using significant M.I.T. funds or facilities, M.I.T. will own the patent, copyright, or other tangible or intellectual property." What constitutes "significant use" is obviously important and open to considerable interpretation, but what is clear is the fact that student innovation, under this particular stipulation, could be wholly owned by the institution. Consequently, students should know in advance what is and what is not possible in the context of their university's policies and procedures. Knowing the requirements and the exceptions to the requirements can help one to avoid running into complicated legal problems after the fact. And in this effort, faculty play a crucial role. It is (or at least should be) the responsibility of faculty to get students to read university policy statements regarding technology transfer and commercialization and to help them understand the practical consequences of these policies for their own work. Although this material is not typically perceived to be part of the curriculum, instructors in all fields and disciplines need to help their students understand both the opportunities and the challenges of their innovation efforts.

Second, students, especially at the undergraduate level, need to begin to think beyond the limitations of the major. The organization of the university into disciplines, each with its own specific degree requirements and set of qualifying criteria, is an administrative convenience useful for allocating resources, processing student throughput, and credentialing graduates. The system, however, is not necessarily useful for students, who may need to draw on and recombine instructional resources from across the institution in the process of responding to new technological opportunities. This is especially true in situations where the principal challenge is not just technological, like machine learning. Take for example, two events from March 2016, Google DeepMind's AlphaGo, which took 4 out of 5 games of Go against one of the most celebrated human players of this notoriously difficult board game, and Tay.ai, a Microsoft Twitterbot that had learned to become a hate-spewing, neo-Nazi racist in less than 8 hours of interaction with human users.

Both AlphaGo and Tay are AI systems that mobilize some aspect of machine learning. AlphaGo, as Google DeepMind (2016) explains it, "combines Monte-Carlo tree search with deep neural networks that have been trained by supervised learning, from human expert games, and by reinforcement learning from games of self-play." In other words, AlphaGo does not play the game by following a set of pre-calculated moves fed into it by human programmers. It is designed to formulate its own instructions from game play. Although less is known about the inner workings of Tay, Microsoft (2016) explains that the system "has been built by mining relevant public data," that is, they trained its neural networks on anonymized information obtained from social media, and that it was designed to evolve its behavior from interacting with users on Twitter, Kik, and GroupMe. What both systems have in common is that the engineers who designed and built them have no idea what the systems will eventually do once they are in operation. As one of the creators of AlphaGo has explained, "Although we have programmed this machine to play, we have no idea what moves it will come up with. Its moves are an emergent phenomenon from the training. We just create the data sets and the training algorithms. But the moves it then comes up with are out of our hands" (Metz 2016).

Responding to the opportunities and challenge made available by mechanisms that do things that are "out of our hands" will require a combination of knowledge and skills that transcend the borders separating what C. P. Snow (1998) described as "the two cultures." Students specializing in one of the technical disciplines will, on the one hand, need to develop the knowledge-base and intellectual skill-set to understand, anticipate, and evaluate the social consequences of the technologies they will be asked to develop and release into the world. This capability cannot be imparted by a single specialized course in "engineering ethics," but will require a much more sustained engagement with the best thinking about the "human condition" as it has been cultivated in art, literature, and philosophy. Likewise, students specializing in one of the "human sciences" need to investigate what this kind of technological innovation means for our concept of the human and the legacy of human exceptionalism. They will need to recognize that information and communication technology are not just tools of human endeavor but, as Luciano Floridi (2014) has described it, a paradigm shattering "fourth revolution" in how we think about ourselves and our place in the world.[2] What is needed, then, to put it in a kind of shorthand formulation, are technology innovators who also understand the profound intricacies of the human condition, and philosophers and artists who can deal with and hack code. Unfortunately, the established structure of the university often discourages this kind of broad interdisciplinary effort. For this reason, and rather than waiting for structural change to trickle down, teachers and students should actively work to remix education by drawing on and repurposing the wide range of resources available within the university structure, even if (and especially if) doing so cuts across boundaries that have been carefully arranged, managed, and protected.

CECI TUERA CELA

From the vantage point of the long tail of history, emerging technologies, especially innovations in information and communication systems, have always confronted existing educational institutions with a significant challenge. Recall, for instance, the introduction of movable type and the printed book. At the time that books were considered "emerging technology," they confronted the established medieval institutions of knowledge production and distribution—which in Europe meant the Catholic Church and its affiliates—with something of an existential crisis. Although there are numerous examinations of the causes and consequences of this transformation in the scholarly literature, one of the more vivid illustrations can be found in Victor Hugo's *Notre-Dame de Paris* (1978, 188): "*Ceci tuera cela*." The statement is attributed to the archdeacon Frollo, and it concerns his rather pessimistic assessment of the impact of Gutenberg's invention: "For some moments the Archdeacon contemplated the gigantic edifice in silence; then, sighing deeply, he pointed with his right hand to the printed book lying open on his table, and with his left to Notre Dame, and casting a mournful glance from the book to the church: 'Alas!' he said. 'This will destroy that'" (Hugo 1978, 188).

The anecdote has been recounted many times not just in the history of print media and technology but also by recent efforts to explain subsequent innovations in information and communication technology, like the personal computer and the Internet (cf. Bolter 2001). But "destroy" is perhaps too strong a word in this context. Obviously, the book did not (literally) raze the gothic edifice. It merely challenged and displaced its function as the principal mode of knowledge production, accumulation, and distribution. Though it may have taken several hundred years, European institutions eventually figured out how to accommodate the technology of print to existing structures and systems. Similarly, the introduction of the personal computer did not put an end to writing, the teaching of composition, or the publication of books. The fact that you are reading about this in a book—whether the letters have been applied to the surface of the pulped flesh of dead trees or are being displayed as intricate patterns of glowing pixels on the screen of a mobile device—is sufficient evidence. Once again, educational institutions learned—and obviously not without some critical hesitation and significant missteps—how to scale the curriculum to the opportunities and challenges of this new technology. Following this precedent, we can anticipate that the current crop of emergent technologies will most probably conform to the contours of this hype cycle. Doing so, however, will require reworking existing educational programs from both ends of the spectrum—developing top-down updates in the structure and operations of the institution and encouraging bottom-up mods that can have an immediate impact on the lives and careers of both teachers and students.

NOTES

1. This approach is deliberate and strategic. In a recent course on AI, Robots, and Communication, I asked my students to investigate the opportunities of emerging technology, the challenges of technological unemployment, and the possible futures for higher education. This effort led to the development of a detailed list of policy initiatives that could be instituted by the university. I had originally intended the exercise to be empowering by giving students the opportunity to reflect on and help shape the direction of their education. But it unfortunately had the exact opposite effect. Looking at the list of reforms, we realized that the proposed updates were well beyond what any of us individually or even in collaboration could possibly achieve. Policy initiatives are certainly important and necessary. But what my students taught me during this semester is that we also need bottom-up strategies that can be instituted immediately in order to respond quickly and directly to the opportunities and challenges students will inevitably face in the next 5 years. It is with this idea in mind, that I dedicate this chapter to my students in COMS 493 at Northern Illinois University, spring of 2016.

2. The term "fourth revolution," which is the title to Floridi's book from 2014, refers to the most recent iteration in a sequence of profound transformations in the way human beings conceive of themselves and the world they occupy. The first revolution, Floridi argues, occurred with Nicholas Copernicus, whose heliocentric model of the solar system challenged human exceptionalism by unseating human beings as the presumptive "center of the universe." The second revolution follows from the work of Charles Darwin, whose theory of evolution demonstrated that the human being was not an exceptional creature

situated apart from the other animals on planet earth but part of a continuum of entities developing out of common ancestors. The third revolution, as Floridi develops it, is attributed to Sigmund Freud, who challenged the notion of Cartesian rationalism and demonstrated that the human mind is not necessarily transparent to itself. The fourth revolution proposed by Floridi is a product of information and communication technology, which has, as he argues, once again reoriented how we think about thought (computational theories of the mind), our bodies (DNA code), and the entire cosmos (infosphere). For a brief introduction, see BBC Radio 4's video "The Fourth Revolution" available at https://www.youtube.com/watch?v=W06fWz1mWNg

REFERENCES

Bolter, Jay David. 2001. *Writing Space: Computers, Hypertext, and the Remediation of Print.* Mahwah, NJ: Lawrence Erlbaum Associates.

Cowburn, Ashley. 2016. Canadian Province Ontario Plans to Trial Universal Basic Income. *Independent*, March 7. http://www.independent.co.uk/news/world/americas/ontario-to-pilot-a-universal-basic-income-experiment-a6916571.html

Diez, Maria Sanchez. 2015. The Dutch 'Basic Income' Experiment is Expanding Across Multiple Cities. *Quartz*, August 13. http://qz.com/473779/several-dutch-cities-want-to-give-residents-a-no-strings-attached-basic-income/

Floridi, Luciano. 2014. *The Fourth Revolution.* Oxford: Oxford University Press.

Ford, Martin. 2015. *Rise of the Robots: Technology and the Threat of a Jobless Future.* New York: Basic Books.

Frey, Carl Benedikt and Michael A. Osborne. 2013. *The Future of Employment: How Susceptible are Jobs to Computerisation?* Oxford Martin School. University of Oxford. http://www.oxfordmartin.ox.ac.uk/publications/view/1314

Google DeepMind. 2016. *AlphaGo.* https://deepmind.com/alpha-go.html

Grove, Jack. 2015. Social Sciences and Humanities Faculties 'To Close' in Japan After Ministerial Intervention. *Times Higher Education*, September 14. https://www.timeshighereducation.com/news/social-sciences-and-humanities-faculties-close-japan-after-ministerial-intervention

Halpern, Sue. 2015. How Robots and Algorithms are Taking Over. *New York Review of Books* 62(6). http://www.nybooks.com/articles/2015/04/02/how-robots-algorithms-are-taking-over/

Hugo, Victor. 1978. *Notre-Dame de Paris* (trans. John Sturrock). New York: Penguin Putnam.

Kenny, Martin, and Donald Patton. 2009. Reconsidering the Bayh-Dole Act and the Current University Invention Ownership Model. *Research Policy* 38: 1407–1422.

162   D.J. GUNKEL

Lorin, Janet. 2016. Student Debt: The Rising US Burden. *Bloomberg*, May 23. http://www.bloomberg.com/quicktake/student-debt
McAfee, Andrew. 2012. Are the Droids Taking our Jobs. *TEDx Boston*, 2012. https://www.ted.com/talks/andrew_mcafee_are_droids_taking_our_jobs
Metz, C. 2016. Google's AI Wins a Pivotal Second Game in Match with Go Grandmaster. *Wired*, March 10. http://www.wired.com/2016/03/googles-ai-wins-pivotal-game-two-match-go-grandmaster/
Microsoft. 2016. Meet Tay—Microsoft A.I. Chatbot with Zero Chill. https://www.tay.ai/
MIT. 2016. *Part 2: MIT Policy Statements.* MIT Technology Licensing Office. http://tlo.mit.edu/community/policies/part2
Pew Research Center. 2014. AI, Robotics, and the Future of Jobs. *Pew*, August. http://www.pewinternet.org/2014/08/06/future-of-jobs/
Popper, Nathaniel. 2016. The Robots Are Coming for Wall Street. *The New York Times*. February 25. http://www.nytimes.com/2016/02/28/magazine/the-robots-are-coming-for-wall-street.html?_r=0
Snow, C.P. 1998. *The Two Cultures.* Cambridge: Cambridge University Press.
Steffensen, Kenn Nakata. 2015. Japan and the Social Sciences: Behind the Headlines. *Times Higher Education*, September 30. https://www.timeshigher-education.com/blog/japan-and-social-sciences-behind-headlines
Sundararajan, Arun. 2016. *The Sharing Economy: The End of Employment and the Rise of Crowd-Based Capitalism.* Cambridge, MA: MIT Press.
Turner, Karen. 2016. Meet 'Ross,' the Newly Hired Legal Robot. *The Washington Post*, May 16. https://www.washingtonpost.com/news/innovations/wp/2016/05/16/meet-ross-the-newly-hired-legal-robot/
Wallach, Wendell. 2015. *A Dangerous Master: How to Keep Technology from Slipping Beyond Our Control.* New York: Basic Books.
White House. 2014. *Taking Action: Higher Education and Student Loan Debt.* http://www.whitehouse.gov/sites/default/files/docs/student_debt_report_final.pdf

Index[1]

[1] Note: Page numbers followed by "n" denote notes.

© The Author(s) 2017
K. LaGrandeur, J.J. Hughes (eds.), *Surviving the Machine Age*,
DOI 10.1007/978-3-319-51165-8